COMPELLING SELLING

SELLING

A FRAMEWORK FOR PERSUASION

PHILIP R. LUND

**A DIVISION OF
AMERICAN MANAGEMENT ASSOCIATIONS**

First published 1974 by THE MACMILLAN PRESS LIMITED, London

Library of Congress Cataloging in Publication Data
Lund, Philip Reginald.
  Compelling selling.
    1. Salesmen and salesmanship.   2. Persuasion (Psychology)
I. Title
HF5438.L747   1975   658.85   74-4748
ISBN 0-8144-5366-1
ISBN 0-8144-7506-X pbk

First AMACOM paperback edition 1978.

Ninth Printing

*To all those who make a
good salesman possible*

Introduction

Most people *sell* every day in their lives. Sometimes what they sell is a product. Sometimes it is an impression they want to give. Usually it is an idea or a course of action. Foremen *sell* to workers. Managers *sell* to employees. Directors *sell* to colleagues on the Board. Husbands *sell* to wives. Accountants, brokers, dentists, and lawyers *sell* to clients. Schoolteachers *sell* to students. And salesmen *sell* to customers.

Most people use sales techniques their mothers taught them when they were children. They learn through experience that it is better to do and say some things than others, without really understanding why. Strangely, in our society, only salesmen are formally taught how to persuade. Consequently, most people spend most of their time upsetting each other, an effect which is usually the exact opposite of the one they are seeking to achieve.

This book attempts to show that all forms of persuasion follow a logical framework and that it is necessary to learn this framework in order to learn the process of successful persuasion. Moreover, a real understanding of the framework helps in interpreting responses correctly and provides a rational medium through which experience can be converted into future action.

All products are either tangible or intangible, and they are sold either directly to the consumer or indirectly to the consumer through a third party.

	Direct	Indirect
Tangible		
Intangible		

Whether you are selling a tangible or intangible *product*, directly or indirectly to the *consumer*, one basic fact remains constant: the common objective in selling all products is to meet your customer's immediate requirements. The skills involved in defining these requirements, in matching your *product* to them, and in causing the customer to reach a decision, are the skills of persuasion. It is with these skills that the book concerns itself.

You are not the exception, so don't kid yourself. The rules of persuasion are the same no matter what you are selling or to whom. The only variations in the many different kinds of *sale* that are made come in the actual shape of the presentation: in the differing emphasis that must be placed within the framework, depending on the product, the customer, and the salesman. Presumably, for example, you would not have too much trouble obtaining an appointment with your wife, although selling the benefits of a course of action to her might take a great deal of time. On the other hand, if you were selling office supplies to an accountant, the situation might be the exact opposite.

In writing this book, it was found necessary to rely almost totally on the salesman's vocabulary. It was impossible to keep repeating, "the persuader persuades the unpersuaded," and the salesman's vocabulary seemed to offer the simplest choice. Partly because of this, and partly because what the salesman does is capable of definition, the decision was made to concentrate the book on the salesman's function.

Similarly, to avoid confusion through too much variety, the examples of dialog in the text are largely confined to one product and to one kind of salesman. Although this must lead to some loss in identification, it provides continuity through the process of the sale and allows the reader to follow the development in the salesman's words and presentation. In reading the book, therefore, where the situation is not your own exactly, try to understand what this salesman does and says, and see if there are any basic lessons in it that apply to you.

One final word about the way this book should be approached. It is designed so that you can open it anywhere and start reading. Each chapter—and as far as possible each section—is self-contained; and to aid in the learning process, there is a certain amount of deliberate repetition. The book is not meant to elaborate every single thought about selling, but to help you generate your own new thoughts and ideas. It is therefore intended not only for those learning to persuade but also as a constant reference for those already well practiced in the skills of persuasion.

From this moment on, whatever the business may be, the persuader will be called the salesman, whatever he sells will be called the product, and whomever he is selling it to will be called the customer. Similarly, the final agreement he seeks to obtain will be called the order whether it is a contract, an order form, or a customer's agreement to specify a product, to contact a contractor for a quotation, to stock a product, to commission a survey, or to take an action. A prospective customer will be called a prospect.

Acknowledgments

My grateful thanks to Jean Aldridge, who gave me so much encouragement in writing this book and who typed the manuscript; to John Drew, Director of the Executive Programmes at the London Business School; to Jim Ringrose, partner of the sales training consultants Ringrose, Higgs & Associates, whose critical appreciation of the draft was so invaluable; and to my dear old mother, without whom even life itself would have been impossible.

Contents

1 The Framework of the Sale

The sale as a sequence of interrelated and logical steps

Selling is the art of communication for persuasion. It is something we all try to do, whether we are selling a load of packaged bread or a highway project to a prospective customer, persuading the financial director to accept our divisional budget, or just breaking a date with the mother-in-law for the weekend without upsetting her. In every case, the rules of persuasion are the same. Too often we fail simply because we do not know them well enough to follow them.

The rules of persuasion are no more than a sequence of clearly defined and interrelated steps. They form a logical framework. Their purpose is to ensure that every point relevant to the negotiation is adequately covered. Furthermore, they provide the dynamic force that will move our prospective customer toward a decision.

If the salesman operates within this framework, he has his greatest chance of success. If he fully understands the framework, he knows exactly where he is in the sale at any one time, and what he must do next. If he neglects any one part, he knows the risk. And if he finally fails to achieve his objective, he knows exactly why.

Selling never has been a matter of being a nice guy, persisting long enough, and relying on the other person to do what is best for himself. For one thing, there are relatively few decisions that are so simple that they offer no alternatives. On the contrary, the salesman must know exactly what he wants to achieve before he starts, must understand what he has to do to achieve it, must go through the rules step by step, and must finally obtain a decision from the person he is seeking to persuade. Obviously, if there are any gaps in his presentation, the sale can slip through and be lost. The result then is failure; and the customer, in accepting the alternative, could well have made the wrong decision.

Most salesmen follow most of the steps that are included in the framework most of the time. They have learned early in life how to go about getting their own way, and this learning is modified through the years by experience. Unfortunately, however, they don't follow some of the steps well and, of course, they don't follow some of them at all. Consequently, what they can do is often made ineffective by what they don't do. And because they themselves do not see the sale as a sequence of logical steps, they rely on luck and gut feeling to guide them. Admittedly, they can be quite successful. On the other hand, it is more effective to know than to feel: to know exactly what you want to achieve, how to set out for it, and what to do next. Then, where you have failed, you have a standard against which your presentation can be compared and adjusted for improvement next time. Otherwise, the method is without control and the presentation progressively collapses. Selling must always be the problem of the one that gets away.

The steps in the sale

The steps in the framework of the sale are really self-explanatory.

PRE-CALL:	Planning to sell
	Identifying the customer
THE SALE:	
Stage 1	Opening the interview
	Getting information
	Establishing the customer's criteria
	for ordering
	Prehandling objections
	Handling competition
	Summarizing for agreement
	(and for trial close)
Stage 2	Selling benefits
	Overcoming objections
	Summarizing prior to closing the sale
Stage 3	Closing the sale
	Keeping the customer sold

Clearly, some of the steps are not so important or so difficult to achieve for some products as for others. However, simple or not, the ground must be covered and the salesman must check that he has successfully achieved each step before going on to the next. Otherwise he will be brought to a halt later with questions he should have covered earlier. As these questions tend to open whole new lines of thought, it might be impossible for him to go back without destroying the structure of his original presentation and, therefore, the dynamics that are moving the prospective customer toward a decision. Once the salesman loses this control, he loses the initiative. The customer in turn might just feel that he has spent enough time on the subject and that there is no further need for him to reconsider his decision. Bang. Out the window goes another sale just because not enough care was taken at the right place and at the right time.

Stage 1 of the framework first requires the salesman to identify the man he must sell to. No amount of talking will sell to the wrong man and, if he finds he has the wrong man, the salesman must stop what he is doing and start his approach again. (The second time it will be that much more difficult.) Only when he has found his way to the decision maker can he open the interview.

Opening the interview requires the salesman to create the level of interest and the physical situation in which business can be discussed. Again, the best salesman in the world will never sell unless he can overcome the problems involved in opening the interview.

When he has won his interview, he must obtain sufficient information through questioning to discover whether the prospective customer is in the market for the exact product or service he is offering. If the customer is in the market, the salesman can proceed. If not, he can only check his findings again and leave.

Having decided that it is worthwhile to continue with the sale, the salesman must establish the specific conditions under which the prospective customer would be prepared to order his product. As the prospective customer will be looking for the best possible solution to his problem, he will inevitably be prepared to make a series of compromises within the broad specifications of his requirements. The salesman now has the opportunity to influence these decision criteria, showing that a small increase in expenditure, for example, will bring a valuable increase in quality. In this way, he can and must match his customer's requirement closely to the product he has to offer. If he fails in this, he will fail in the sale and there is therefore no point in going further.

Once this is achieved, he must obtain agreement that these are in fact the only criteria that need to be satisfied in the decision. If they are not, he must go back again, adding and modifying criteria until he has the complete picture of the benefits the customer is seeking from the new product or service. Any omissions now will disrupt and possibly destroy the sale at a later stage.

After reaching agreement on decision criteria, the salesman must handle competition: that is, the alternative courses of action the customer can take, from choosing a competitor's product to simply doing nothing. This he does by confirming the importance of the criteria they have agreed upon—which match his product—and by showing how important it is that the decision be made.

He must now prehandle the objections that he knows from experience will give the prospective customer the opportunity of avoiding a decision. To do this, he identifies objections one by one with the customer and agrees that they will not constitute obstacles at the time of the final decision.

Now all he has to do to complete Stage 1 of the sale is to summarize again the agreements they have made between them, and *trial close:*

> "If I can provide the product that will satisfy these criteria, will you place your order with me?"

The customer can hardly say no. After all, it was he who listed the criteria in the first place.

During Stage 1, discussion is centered on the customer's problem. This creates the basis on which the sale is made. The product or service is barely mentioned. Stage 2, however, now shows how the customer's requirements are satisfied by the product.

In selling benefits, the salesman shows that the benefits his product offers match exactly the benefits the customer is seeking. This is usually a question of evidence substantiated by visual aids, third-party references, and demonstration.

Once the customer can agree that the product does satisfy his requirements, the salesman must now overcome his outstanding objections. As most of the objections to taking action have already been prehandled, the objections at this stage will be largely operational in nature and will be covered by the salesman through his knowledge of the physical characteristics and purchase conditions of his product. Now all he has to do is resummarize the conclusions they agreed upon during benefit selling, prior to closing the sale.

Stage 3, the close, is the logical conclusion to the negotiation. The customer has outlined what he wants, the salesman has shown that his product satisfies this requirement, and, together, they have agreed that there is no reason why the decision should not be taken immediately. The salesman therefore asks for the decision and, if he has covered the ground properly, the customer can only say yes. The contract, if there is one, is signed.

Now, with the order in his pocket, the salesman's remaining problem is to keep his customer sold. This basically means keeping him happy in his decision throughout the years of their association. Otherwise, competition will gain a foothold, and it is a truism in selling that it is much more difficult to win back a lost customer than to find a new one.

Besides his direct contact with the customer, there are all the pre-call activities in which a good salesman must involve himself. This is the salesman's constant business, preparing himself and improving his presentation so that he does not make obvious mistakes, planning his territory both geographically and in terms of types of customer so that time is used effectively, and identifying and redefining specific sales objectives so that no opportunity is lost. It is the hard work behind every sale, and without it the salesman cannot be successful.

The use of questions in selling

The No. 1 rule of human communication is: *People prefer talking to listening.* Look at it from your own experience. Who is the more interesting person to talk with, the one who talks intelligently about a number of different subjects while you listen, or the one who asks you a number of intelligent questions and listens to what you have to say? There is no doubt about it, is there?

The ability to ask questions is the sine qua non of successful selling. Without questions you can never find out what the prospective customer wants to buy, or even if he wants to buy anything. It is for want of good questions that poor salesmen find their presentations falling a mile wide of the mark.

What are the real advantages of questions?

Questions allow you to retain the initiative in the discussion. Obviously, if you are asking the questions, you hold the right to establish the subject under discussion. Similarly, the conversation will continue along the lines indicated by your questioning.

Questions give you control of the conversation. Just as you can influence the lines along which the conversation develops, so you can change the subject under discussion the moment you feel the conversation is heading in the wrong direction. Then, if you want the person to stop talking altogether, all you need do is ask a question that expects a yes or no answer. Even interrupting to ask this question will cause no upset.

Questioning makes you appear a pleasant and interesting person, on the principle that people prefer talking to listening. If you have enough questions, they will go on talking all day. As night falls and you manage to escape to another destination, they will still have the energy to say, "What a nice person that was and what an interesting conversation." Try it and see for yourself!

Questions allow you to adapt your conversation and modes of expression to the characteristics of the person you are talking to. To sell well you do not have to try to change your class or status. You just have to ask the right questions, listen to the way the customer expresses himself, and reply using the same terms. It is when you talk rather than listen, and use terms of expression that are unfamiliar to the customer, that misunderstanding occurs and communication is lost.

Questions also clarify and elucidate. Few people can express an idea fully in one or two sentences. Most people in conversation leave a lot to the imagination of their listener. (Remember this next time someone tries to describe a film or a television program to you.) No good salesman can take the risk of misunderstanding from incomplete information, so he must constantly check the meaning with questions.

Questions beginning HOW, WHY, WHEN, WHERE, WHAT, WHO require a qualifying response and it is these that clarify meaning and establish understanding.

Questions can be used to establish commitment. Obviously every salesman seeks to commit his prospective customer to a favorable decision, and the technique he uses is based on the conditional sentence:

"If I . . . , will you . . . ?"

In selling it is known as the *trial close*, and it is a key question in any sale. Basically it says:

> "*If we* can agree on what you want, and *if I* can show you that I can give it to you, *will you* make a decision in my favor?"

As it is vital in the sale to obtain commitment, so it is important in any form of persuasion that seeks to modify behavior.

We can see therefore that questions are as essential to the sale as they are to every other form of persuasion. If you want to learn to sell, and you don't know where to start, this is your first lesson: *Learn to ask questions.* There is only one way to do it, and that is by doing it. Try to go for a day making no statements but only asking questions. Then do it again. It will become progressively easier. See for yourself how well you can make yourself understood by using questions in place of statements. There is not a statement that cannot be expressed as a question, even if all you can do is put the words "isn't it" at the end of the sentence, or "surely" at the beginning. If you have the will to do this, you will quickly learn to restructure the way you communicate with people. And even while you do it, you will notice the change in their response to you. You will become a better persuader.

A top-flight salesman can carry through the whole sale from beginning to end, making no statements and using only questions. You will really know how to ask questions if you can do the same.

Remember Kipling:

> I keep six honest serving-men
> (They taught me all I knew);
> Their names are WHAT and WHY and WHEN
> And HOW and WHERE and WHO.*

Selling as a logical process to achieve an emotional objective

How many times have you tried to persuade a friend to drop some course of action he is planning? You have proved to him conclusively that what he intends to do can end only in disaster. Try as you may, he shows little interest in your arguments and goes ahead with his plan.

* From "The Elephant's Child," *Just-So Stories.*

All the results you foretold come about—yet even then he is unrepentant.

The basic problems you had in persuading lay in your approach. You assumed that logical arguments would prevail so you piled them up in your support. The result was that you did not persuade him to change his action. Instead you probably compounded his resolve to carry on with it. You achieved this because what you really succeeded in telling him was that you thought he was wrong; and the more you proved he was wrong, the less chance you gave him of saving face and accepting your solution.

Few people are prepared to admit openly that they are just plain wrong. Most people will, however, accept that there is an alternative possibility; and they will even be persuaded by it if they feel that the arguments support it. This is one instance in which we can see the sale determined by emotional rather than logical criteria. Logic is used in marshaling and presenting the substantive evidence. The decision to make a new decision, however, is very much emotionally based.

The purpose of treating the sale within a methodical framework is to allow countervailing views to be presented without meeting this blind resistance. It does so through a questioning technique that asks the respondent—the prospective customer—first to define his problem in his own words and then to list the criteria that he feels must be satisfied in its solution. This puts the respondent at ease. It is his problem that is being discussed and it is his opinion that is being invited. He does most of the talking. It also puts the questioner psychologically on the side of the respondent by indicating his interest and his willingness to assist.

This is how the respondent sees the situation. In fact, it is the questioner who controls the content of the conversation by controlling the questions that are asked. Through these questions, he can begin to influence the respondent by introducing the other factors that he thinks are relevant to the decision. Soon it is not difficult for him to agree with the respondent on a decision plan that will have the alternative action as the solution to the respondent's problem.

Another moment at which the sale is influenced by the emotional rather than the logical is at the point of decision itself. No one likes making decisions. They take away the choice of alternative action and, particularly in the business world, they tend to cost money. Remember from your own experience how difficult and upsetting it is sometimes to write checks to pay simple bills—even when you have the money! So it is with most decisions and, if possible, people would prefer to leave them until tomorrow.

On the other hand, a few people like decisions hanging over them. A good decision taken brings with it a sense of relief because it puts the problem to bed. Also, it is frustrating to discuss a problem with somebody at length without reaching a conclusion.

The way the framework of the sale handles this paradox is by requiring an early commitment to the decision from the respondent. This raises the emotional content of the dialog and prepares the way for a decision to be made. The framework then logically removes any possibility of alternative action, proves that the proffered solution satisfies the decision criteria, and demands a decision. At this point, the good salesman is silent. He uses silence to force the prospective customer to overcome his emotional reluctance and to make his decision. Once he has made his decision, however, particularly where the salesman has been thorough in handling his doubts and questions, the new customer will feel a considerable sense of relief.

Whatever the form of persuasion, no decision is ever made unless it is explicitly demanded and given. If you leave without actually asking for the decision, the chances are that your respondent has emotionally avoided making one.

2 Planning to Sell

Personal preparation

A good salesman has qualities of

> intelligence
> perception
> self-motivation
> enthusiasm
> integrity
> discipline
> resilience
> self-criticism
> ambition to succeed

He needs intelligence to grasp the sales problem and to talk at the level of his customer. If he cannot establish communication at this level, he will never sell.

He needs perception so that he can identify and understand the customer's problem. The good salesman sells what the customer requires rather than what he says he wants.

He needs self-motivation to generate continually the new ideas and the enthusiasm necessary for making sales. It is this kind of *persistence* that a good salesman will have.

He needs enthusiasm to be able always to see his product as he would want his customer to see it. Sales management obviously has a vital role in reinforcing his attitude.

Integrity is needed if only because it is through the salesman that the company is seen. Business is concerned with satisfied customers. Customer deception and customer satisfaction are obviously antithetical.

The good salesman needs discipline for three main reasons: to control his territory and to work it according to his territory plan; to control himself, the words he uses, and the things he says; and to control his customer so that the sale proceeds logically from introduction to decision. Discipline is the single most important determinant of sales ability.

He needs resilience so that he can capitalize on his success during good times and not lose sight of the real benefits of his product during bad times.

He needs self-criticism so that he can constantly review his performance and raise its level. He must learn to hate his mistakes and to improve. Mediocrity is a heavy burden for any man to carry.

Finally, he must have the ambition to succeed. This will give him the energy and drive necessary to overcome the possibility of failure.

The salesman's first responsibility is to prepare himself. He is a professional. He should think of himself as a professional, behave like a professional, and be treated like a professional.

Before he goes out on a territory he should be properly trained. Training should include the basic rules of selling, knowledge of his own and competing products, market orientation on the opportunity to practice a balanced oral presentation in company with others, and encouragement.

It is important that he not be thrown into the field with too little knowledge and experience, and damaged. The first three months are the most important in developing the salesman's attitude to his job. his product, and his company.

The salesman should wear clean pressed clothes and clean shoes. If he hasn't that much respect for himself, he cannot expect others to have it for him. He should look as good or better than the man he is talking to. Appearance suggests competence.

He should not stand out with bright ties, long hair, or fancy clothes and shoes. If anything he wears or does upsets one person, it upsets one person too many. It is not a question of right or wrong. The order is lost and the objection may never be heard. The man has just decided not to do business with him.

Shabby clothes and shabby habits cause loss of confidence and loss of orders. The shabby, ill-disciplined, good salesman sells in spite of himself. How much better he would do if he improved his manners.

Similarly, no one wants to do business with a salesman who is pessimistic, indifferent, scared, or inefficient.

The man who calls smelling of beer is wrong. So is the man who smokes from the moment he enters the customer's office. Of course the customer says yes, you can smoke. It is not what he says that matters, it is what he thinks. The salesman must play the part and not throw away his opportunity.

He should eat regularly, sleep regularly, and go on regular holidays. These are important in successful selling. If he sets high personal standards for himself, he will be a winner. If he cannot sell and lead a normal life, he should get out of the profession before he dies of poverty or a heart attack.

He should go to bed at reasonable hours. He may have one chance to take an order tomorrow, and he cannot afford to miss it because he has been playing around all night. That can be left for the weekends. Selling is a hard professional business, and the prizes and rewards go to the man with a hard professional attitude.

The salesman should maintain his professional and trade knowledge by regularly reading professional and trade books and pamphlets. No one has complete knowledge, and a hint from today's reading can produce tomorrow's sale. Selling the extra unit is a question of being able to recognize the extra opportunity.

He should study the industry where there is no market for his product at the moment but where there perhaps could be. He must not waste selling time but should look for the trick that will put his product into a new industry. In selling there is a fortune to be made by doing what the other man has not done.

He can also learn by calling on his existing customers. It will help him to stay in touch with their thinking, their problems, and the ways they are using his product—and they will be glad to see him too.

It is good practice for a salesman to review one selling rule each week. When you work alone on a territory it is too easy to become inflexible and to reduce your presentation until it becomes meaningless. Don't wait until the orders fall off: *Keep to the rule of practice.* It is the one major expansive exercise that the salesman can carry out on his own.

The salesman should consider that he has one chance, and one chance only, to take the order. The wrong word, the wrong action, and he has thrown that chance. It is always more difficult to go back later than to do the job properly in the first place.

The optimum presentation has the fewest words and the fewest actions. More are superfluous and only place the salesman at an additional risk of losing the order.

A salesman must watch his own performance and judge it objectively. He must continually criticize his approach, the path he takes, the words he uses. Even when he has won the order, there have been words he has used dangerously and attitudes he has taken wrongly. If he can learn a little from each presentation, he will improve.

It can help the salesman if he will write up a scenario for his presentation and memorize it. He can do this in his own time. Then when he comes under pressure, he will not hesitate and forget the important benefits.

Overfamiliarity with his own presentation, on the other hand, can influence the salesman's judgment of what is and what is not important in his presentation. What may seem irrelevant to the salesman after a thousand presentations may be extremely relevant to the customer who is hearing the presentation for the first time.

One opportunity to evaluate the balance, emphasis, and omissions in the salesman's presentation comes from discussions with his field sales manager while they are making calls together. If your field sales manager is too lazy to do this, arrange to spend one day a month in the field with a colleague. You will always find this dialog stimulating.

The salesman should appear an interesting and competent businessman. First impressions are lasting impressions. He must be a man of the world, with reading in literature and current events, and an acquaintance with the theater, opera, and art. These interests are available to everyone: few make any use of them.

The salesman must appear at least as good as the man to whom he is selling. Knowledge and ability are always respected. There is no advantage in reducing yourself to the level of the man you are talking to, or in raising yourself above him. Orders are not won that way. It looks wrong and it is wrong. The only game you can play convincingly is your own game.

Finally, in selling, as we have seen, the decision to sign is emotional even when the reasons to buy are logical. The salesmen who can sell are therefore the salesmen who can motivate. Personal preparation should make the factors that motivate a primary consideration.

Producing a product is one problem; selling it is another. The sales problem must be absorbed. Otherwise, the market just learns to like the mice rather than search out the company with the mousetrap.

The difference in terms of productivity between an ordinary salesman and a good salesman is plus 100 percent. The difference between a good salesman and a brilliant salesman is plus another 100 percent. How good are you?

Product knowledge

The customer buys a product for the benefits it will bring him and the problems it will solve for him, rather than for what it is. The salesman, however, must know what his product is so that he can know exactly what it does. Only then can he sell the real benefits of what it does.

He must know completely and exactly the benefits of his products for each category of customer. He will not use every benefit for every customer. He would be wrong to do so. He must be able to identify the category of customer with whom he is negotiating and bring forward appropriately the two or three critical benefits. Before he can do this, he must know every benefit.

He must know how the products work. Total technical knowledge is not usually necessary in selling a product. He must know only as much as he needs to answer the questions the customer asks. If the customer continues to pursue technical detail beyond the point where it proves the product's ability to perform its function, the salesman is probably either selling to the wrong person or selling the product in the wrong way.

What is important is that the product is capable of doing what it is said to do. A short, clear, explicit statement of how it does so is sufficient to prove capability in most cases. Technical discussion tends to emphasize the detail of what the product is rather than the solutions and benefits it will provide. Too much stress on technical detail may bring admiration and applause, but it is unlikely to bring sales.

The salesman must know the major users of his company's products by industry, and their experience. These are the good references for his product. He must also know how they carry out their business so that he can know the questions he should be asking similar companies.

He must know about new developments in his own products and new end uses that have been uncovered for them. It is a management job to make sure that he has this information firsthand.

He must have knowledge of future company products. When he has been beaten by his competitors, it is his only weapon. It is a poor alternative to sell what he *will* have rather than what he has, but it is better than losing a customer altogether.

The salesman must know details of the services his company offers—repairs, resupply, technical support, training, subsidiary products. These can be the major benefits he has to offer and the factors that really differentiate his product from others.

He must know his own company, its history, its paid-up capital, its financial record, its senior officers, its position in the market, its subsidiary operations, and its foreign associations. He must be in a position to answer questions.

He must know whom he can go to and for what. And what he needs must be there for him. He must be totally supported in the field. He must not have the feeling that he is fighting for his company in the field and against his company in the office.

He must know how he is paid and when. This is vital. Money is an important motivation.

He must be encouraged continually. He works on his own and lives with problems. He does not telephone his office to hear what he has *not* done—he telephones to be loved, and that is a selling job for his sales manager. He does not come into the office to fill in forms—he comes in to be encouraged, to gain the strength he needs to go back out into the field.

He must know the team to which he belongs, his sales branch, and his sales district. These are the people he identifies and competes with. He must be brought together with them regularly for meetings and training.

He must know how he stands in relation to his colleagues in sales. He must be placed in competitive situations where success is rewarded. He must be kept up to date with the progress of any competition and celebrated with any prize. Nothing is worse and more negative than a competition no one cares about.

The salesman must know everything about his competitors that he knows about his own company. It is no use being surprised with competitive information from a customer. The salesman must know what the customer is going to say and be prepared with the answer.

He must know what the competitors' products do, how they do it, and their comparative benefits. If a competitor has and will have overwhelming benefits in the market the salesman is selling to, then it could be time to change sides.

He must know the advantages of competitive products so that he can fully understand the real benefits his products offer. Similarly, he must know the services his competitors have to offer.

He must know why his competitors' customers prefer their products, even if it means calling on these customers to find out.

The salesman must be convinced of the benefits of his own products. It is an unusually bad product that does not offer some particular and worthwhile benefit.

No salesman should have to be sold his product before he can sell it. He will sell it to himself as he sees it solving customers' problems. On the other hand, the salesman must be able to see that even under the most trying circumstances the company is doing what it can to keep his customers happy. Otherwise he will lose faith and, without that faith, he will not sell.

Don't moan and groan every time something goes wrong with your product or with delivery. No one's product is perfect or ever will be. Do what you can to solve the problem and keep firmly and clearly at the front of your mind the real benefits the customer gains from using your product.

Remember that all products are different, even if the differences are only in the men selling them. So be different, and be better. Make sure that you are the most desirable person for the customer to do business with. It can make up for a lot of deficiencies in the product.

Remember also that, as the customer is buying the product for what it will do for him, his opinion of you will influence his opinion of the product. He knows that sooner or later he is going to have problems with the product and, when he does, he wants to know that he can rely on you to solve them.

Whatever the advantages or disadvantages of your product, make a point of assessing and understanding your customer's problems, and look for new and better ways to show him how your product meets his requirements. There is nothing more deadly than a salesman who tells the same old story.

Be creative. When you have an idea, try to *explode* it. Try to discover what is good about it and how it can best be used. Then you will develop it. If you only concentrate on its problems, all you will end up with is good reasons for doing nothing, or nothing new.

The sales plan

A salesman's *sales plan* is his company's total annual sales plan, divided by the number of salesmen, divided by the number of months or weeks in the year.

If the salesman does not have a sales plan, he does not know what he is doing. If the manager does not know the salesman's sales plan, he does not know what the salesman is doing; and he probably does not know what he is doing himself.

Without a sales plan, a salesman has no guide. Without a sales plan, the sales manager can give him no guidance.

Before he can make a meaningful sales plan, the salesman must know the *sales cycle* for his product and his *conversion rate* for business. The sales cycle is the average number of calls he must make to each category of customer to take an order, and the conversion rate is the average number of new calls he must make to win a new order from a new customer.

The sales plan will specify the average income to be earned by the average salesman for average work. It describes the minimum expected performance. Actual performance at this level is not particularly good for either the salesman or the company.

The sales plan is based on an annual objective satisfactory to both the salesman and the sales supervisor. It must be a marriage of the company's requirement and the salesman's requirement. It should among other things establish what each will require of the other in the way of orders, demonstration facilities, product availability, servicing, and technical support.

The annual objective must be broken down into acceptable meaningful units, probably sales per month, possibly sales per week. These then provide the yardstick by which the salesman can measure his progress toward his annual target.

The salesman looks at his monthly objective as the target he can reach and surpass. Low targets encourage laziness, high targets hopelessness. The target should be possible with effort and direction. The sales manager's function is to show the salesman how his target can be achieved.

The salesman inevitably has a choice of ways to achieve his sales targets. Often, for example, he can choose between taking more smaller orders and fewer larger orders. Choose the easiest way to achieve your target, the one that will involve you in least risk. Let yourself be influenced by the way you can make most money out of the company incentive scheme.

If you have a monthly sales objective, make sure you achieve it monthly. Don't kid yourself that you will take the orders next month. You won't. You'll fall behind.

A *new customer* is a customer the company has not done business with before. He represents new business. Existing customers and new customers must be considered separately by both the salesman and the sales manager. The salesman the company must love is the one who brings in new customers. It is in these customers that the company has real growth potential.

The salesman must judge existing customers and new customers in terms of their order-producing potential. His priority must be to take orders.

No salesman needs to think he will take fewer orders than any other. The worse his conversion rate and the more calls he makes to take an order, the harder he will have to work and the better planning he must do. The better the salesman, the less he needs to do to produce the same results and the more time he has to produce increasingly more business and increasingly more wealth.

A good salesman gets up in the morning knowing exactly what he is going to do. He has planned ahead.

Between 9 A.M. and 5 P.M. he must run the risk of taking orders through face-to-face contact with customers. Between 9 A.M. and midday he should make the calls where the decisions are critical and perhaps telephone for appointments. This is the prime selling time. Complaining customers can be left till 4 P.M., when they are too tired to talk, or 5 P.M., when they want to go home.

Between 5 P.M. and 9 A.M., the salesman can do the things that do not require the customer to be there. He can write letters, fill out reports, send out mailshots (that is, direct-mail advertising) for windfall business, research his territory, and plan. If he works in the field fully between 9 A.M. and 5 P.M., he will have only just enough time between 5 P.M. and 9 A.M. to cover his administration.

There are no special prizes for salesmen who call at 8 A.M. or 6 P.M. or on Saturdays, unless the customer wants to see him then. The weekends should be set aside for enjoyment and relaxation.

Set your appointments on the quarter hours. If you think you could be a little late, tell your customer so. If you find you are running a little late, telephone before the time of your appointment to say when you will arrive. The customer can understand that sometimes you will be a little late, but he may not forgive your bad manners if you fail to forewarn him.

The salesman is running a small business in his territory. He should treat his territory that way and be treated that way.

If the salesman is allowed to become dependent on his manager, he will learn to rely on him for running his territory and will be lost without him. He must be forced to be independent. If he cannot make decisions, his customers never will.

Lunchtime, so the story goes, is a good time to canvass because the usual people are out to lunch and names are easier to come by. Leave that one until you have a problem in getting a name. Your sales plan should include arrangements for a normal life—normal meals, social activity, sleep. If you cannot work successfully and lead a normal life, then you should change your job.

Truth to tell, and unhappily for most salesmen, mind ultimately produces more business than physical strength. Think it out properly first; but then make sure you do something about it.

The scarcity in selling is time. Take orders as quickly as you can, see as many customers as you can, and spend selling time selling. The first customer to visit is the one who will give you his order. See him first.

If you know how long it takes to obtain an order from each category of customer, then you know how much time you must give a customer before taking his order. You must get started on slow business as soon as you take a new territory, and, if you sell to government agencies, you must program your work to their budget dates.

You will learn the typical pattern of calls to take an order: cold call, demonstration, quotation, follow-up call. You will gain a shrewd idea of the number of customers you will need in negotiation at any one time to keep the order pipeline flowing. All you have to do now is put the information to useful purpose. And you should plan it by numbers.

Establish the *number* of face-to-face contacts you need each week to achieve and surpass your sales target. No salesman ever took orders sitting at his desk, unless his customer came to him.

Establish the *number* of customer calls you must make to maintain existing business, to maximize repeat business, and to keep in touch with user thinking.

Establish the *number* of cold calls you must make to gain new prospective customers at the required rate.

Establish the *number* of new prospective customers it takes to feed the right number of hot prospective customers into the order pipeline.

Establish the *number* of demonstrations or quotations you must complete in a week to transform interested prospects into excited hot prospects.

Establish the *number* of hot prospects you must have on your list to yield the number of orders that matches your weekly target. All your other calls must now be geared to replace the wastage from this list.

Make it your responsibility to formalize these requirements as figures on a piece of paper. Then compare them week by week. It is only when they are seen in comparison with each other week by week that you can see whether they work together, how they work together, and what you can do to the mix to make them work together better. Doing it is what counts.

Finally, if you reach your weekly target by Wednesday, do not start preparing for next week's orders. Try to take them before Friday.

The territory plan

Essentially, a salesman is running a small business on his own. He judges his market, adapts his presentation to it, sells to it and arranges delivery, creates new end uses for his products, and profits by the commission paid on his activity.

The only way a small business can be run properly is through planning. A territory must be planned by geographical area, by category of customer, and by customer ordering date.

The first thing to do is to buy a map and have a look at your area. Draw in the boundary. Drive around the area and see what you can of it. Get a feel for it. It is too easy at the start of a new year to sit in your office, study hard, and dream about the orders you will take. Orders come only from face-to-face contact.

Take an annual view of your market. Worry about orders you will take this year, and let the orders you will take next year look after themselves. Your company survives on orders now, not on the promises of orders in the future.

Find out where the existing customers for your products are. The chances are that your new customers will be in the same area as well. Certainly this is the market area for any complementary products you offer and the place where you are going to feel the breeze of competition most strongly.

Define the characteristics of existing customers—size, markets, methods, problems—and see if there are any businesses with the same characteristics elsewhere in the area. They could have the same ordering potential.

Take care that the spread of your existing customers has not been determined only by the efforts of a previous lazy salesman. Pick out the industrial areas with the greatest business density. You do not want to spend too many afternoons floating around the countryside—unless you are an agricultural products salesman or the weather is good.

Divide the territory into areas that can be worked economically in time and effectively in coverage. Make a provisional assessment of the time you will need to spend in each area during the week and the month, and write it down.

If your territory is too large, tell your management. There is no advantage to a large territory if you have to dilute your effort. You will end up with nothing.

Take the previous salesman's *hot* prospective customer list and try to close the sales immediately. Most of the prospects will in fact be duds because he will have done everything in his power to close the sales, but you cannot afford to miss a chance.

The previous salesman's records, with the exception of customer and hot prospect lists, are usually not helpful. Somewhere they will contain the reason why he did not get the order. It could be a matter of the wrong name. A fresh approach may do the trick. Look through them by all means, but do not spend any time with them. Generally, they only bring harm.

The man who follows a poor salesman is going to have his work cut out building up the momentum of the territory again. Every salesman thinks he has exhausted a territory when he has finished. Yet next year it is producing again, and usually at twice the rate.

Territories have this interesting characteristic: the better they are worked, the better they work next time. This is the strongest argument for changing sales territories each year.

The good salesman will estimate the ordering potential for each category of customer. He will then apportion his time to correspond to this potential.

The apportioned amount of time will be increased or decreased for each category of customer according to the level of penetration and the degree of difficulty in taking the order.

Spend more time in those areas where it is easier and quicker to take the order, but understand the risk. The more time you spend in one area, the less time you spend in another, and the more susceptible that area will be to the inroads of competition. Also, the market segment that is slow in the short term could contain important potential for the near future.

For existing customers, find out from your territory records exactly what each customer is using and in what quantity. Find out why similar businesses are not using similar products in a similar way. There may well be opportunities here.

Companies in a similar business, or companies using the product in a similar way, constitute similar markets.

Make it a question of priority to call on existing customers during your early days on a new territory. They will welcome your visit and they are a source of immediate repeat business, new orders, user experience, third-party references, and competitive information. Ask them which competitors are approaching them and how.

The good salesman will also balance his workload between long-term prospects, medium-term prospects, and short-term prospects. They must all be worked together so that they fill the order pipeline in turn at a steadily increasing rate.

Make an initial decision on long-term prospects. If a category of customer takes six months from introduction to order and you want the business in six months' time, you must begin the contact now. Here a mailshot could be used to cream off the top percentage of those *definitely interested.*

Long-term prospects often have multi-order potential, which is important in providing basic bread-and-butter business.

Time must also be allotted to medium-term prospects and the decision made whether to cover the whole market area or concentrate on specific sections. Remember again, however, that what you don't do the competition is likely to do.

Short-term prospects must be approached right away and the maximum amount of time must be devoted to them. By definition, they have decided they want to make a decision in the short term and have, therefore, become vulnerable to competition.

The productive salesman plans his time and territory to maximize his return over the short, medium, and long term. It is not the time spent on a call, or even the number of calls you make, that matters: it is the business you bring in.

There are four ways to increase the amount of business you do:

Increase the effective selling time available to you.

Increase the number of effective selling calls you make.

Reduce the number of calls you make to any one customer in order to take his order.

Improve your rate of converting new prospective customers to new orders.

Anything you do to improve your performance in these areas will require planning.

Set the basic framework of a day's calls by telephoning for appointments. Then each day you will know at least the type of customers you will be seeing, the category of calls you will be making, and where you will be making them. Canvassing and cold calls can then fill the time between arranged calls.

The sales pattern

Every sale should have the following pattern:

Interest — when the prospective customer wants to discuss his problem

Desire — when he wants to accept your solution

Close — when he finalizes his decision

Interest must always precede desire in the sale. Interest is created by the customer talking about himself and his problems. The product is barely mentioned.

Desire is created by benefit selling, during which the salesman talks about his product in the terms the customer used to describe his problem and shows how the product provides the solution to the problem.

The final close is the question the salesman uses to ask the customer to make his decision. It can come anywhere in the sale from the first sentence on:

"Would you like one?"

It is unlikely that the salesman will lose the sale by trying to close it too often. On the other hand, he will certainly lose the sale if he does not close. Therefore, a salesman should always make a point of closing the sale at least once every interview, however hopeless it looks.

Every sale has a primary objective which must be closed. This is to take the order. Each contact or call you make will have a secondary objective which must be closed, for example, to set an appointment. These are the steps you must complete in order to achieve the final objective. The progress toward both primary and secondary objectives, however, must always follow the path *interest, desire, close*. There are no exceptions.

Whether you are telephoning, writing, calling, or demonstrating, you must hit the customer's interest the first time. If you fail, there is every chance that he will put down the telephone on you, tear up your letter, turn you out, tell you that your product is useless, or tell you not to bother him.

Immediate impact is essential. You must always know what you are going to say before you say it. If you stutter, stumble, or hesitate, you may well lose his interest and his business.

One way is to be interesting yourself. Sound as though you have something worth hearing. You must work out your style yourself. Certainly always sound enthusiastic about what you have to say. If *you* can't be enthusiastic, no one else is going to be.

Another way is to ask the right question. If the question is right, the customer will come back with an interested answer. That question could easily come from something you see on his premises or something you know about his business.

Another way is to make a statement that will cause him to ask a question. Once he has asked the question, even the hardest man will wait and listen to the answer, and you have the opportunity to catch his interest.

Once you have gained his interest in talking to you, you must convert it into an interest in discussing his problem with you. At this point the sale is under way. The customer is persuaded to detail the criteria he needs to satisfy by his decision.

Desire for the product develops during benefit selling as the prospective customer becomes convinced that the product being offered will provide the solution to his problem. He begins to want it and what it will do for him. It is the point at which, with the evidence before him, he makes an emotional commitment that will propel him inevitably to a final decision. This commitment is strengthened as the salesman asks, for example:

"How do you see this benefit helping you?"

"What kind of saving could this give?"

"How much worry would this save you?"

The customer becomes involved in his own decision. It becomes important for him to make a decision.

The customer is now more than logically involved in the buying decision. Everything must be done to increase the emotional content of the sale without breaking its continuity: questions, word pictures, visual aids, third-party references, attractive reasonable proposals which ease the decision, demonstrations. If the right pressure is applied in the right way to the emotional side of a person's nature, success is assured. The sale will move on from the desire stage to the close.

It is essential that the salesman retain tight control at this stage. The primary objective is the order. The customer must be moved relentlessly to the point where he will sign.

But the customer will take the first way out to flee from his sense of mounting pressure. The salesman must remove any opportunity for escape. He must be careful not to be tempted by his own control and by the customer's enthusiasm into saying too much, thereby unbalancing his presentation, reducing the pressure, and perhaps losing the order. He must cover fully all the points relevant to the customer's decision criteria and, the moment he has the customer's agreement that all the points have been covered, he must close firmly.

If the job had been properly done, the only thing left for the customer to say is yes.

The sales cycle

Some orders come in quickly, some a bit more slowly, and some a lot more slowly. Overall, there is an average time in which the salesman can reasonably expect to take the order. This is his *sales cycle.*

The sales cycle is the average number of calls the salesman makes to turn a new contact into a new order. Obviously the average number of calls needed to take an order can also be expressed as an average amount of time.

In his planning, the salesman takes into account the number of calls he expects to make to win the order. When he exceeds that number, he knows something is wrong.

New business comes from new customers. The number of new orders you take will be related directly to the size of your reservoir of new prospective customers.

Repeat orders for the same product and new orders for new products come from existing customers. These should already be yours. Real growth comes from new business and therefore from new customers.

New prospects (*new prospective customers*) are obtained from new calls. Each week should contain the right number of new calls. The right number is assessed by the length of the sales cycle for each category of customer and by the planning requirements for feeding these customers into the order pipeline.

In the course of the sales cycle, a new contact will become a new prospect, then a hot prospect, then a new order.

Most of your new contacts should become new prospects. Otherwise the chances are that you are defining your market improperly and calling on the wrong companies. You should call only on contacts who seem likely, from your experience, to be a market for your product.

If you are a good salesman and can convert one new prospect in three into an order, and you know how many calls you must make to any one customer to take his order, you have the basis for a sales plan to achieve your weekly and monthly targets.

If you know your rate of converting prospects to orders and the number of calls you must make to take the order, then you can estimate the number of hot prospects you will need at any one time to achieve a weekly order rate that will match your target.

If you are selling a range of products, then you will need a hot prospect list for each category of product. If you are selling products by volume or value, you will need a hot prospect list that will give you the required orders.

If you exhaust three hot prospects to take one order, your sales plan will require the creation of three new hot prospects during the same period to maintain your production at a constant level. Three new hot prospects could mean eight new proposals which become hot at differing rates. Eight new prospects could require ten new contacts in a week.

The sales plan will include new calls, new prospects, hot prospects, new orders, and knowledge of the conversion rate and the sales cycle for your product. Experience will show you what you will need in the reservoir to keep the order pipeline flowing.

In addition to initial and follow-up calls on new prospects, you must make calls to existing customers to keep repeat orders flowing in at an increasing rate. It is always more difficult to win back a customer you have lost than to find a new one.

The optimum sales cycle must be based on the performance of the best salesman in the company. This is the basis on which the sales cycles of the other salesmen can be judged.

If a salesman has a long sales cycle, then he must be compared in performance and method to the more productive salesman. If he is worth his salt, he will persuade this more successful—but not necessarily better—salesman to go out on his territory with him.

What he can learn from this salesman is the particular skill in selling the product that increases the success rate and reduces the selling time. To sell more effectively, he needs to discover which physical characteristics in the product to emphasize, and which arguments to use when presenting these characteristics to the customer. The successful salesman has this *trick:* it can be identified and copied.

A cold call can increase the sales cycle by one call. The salesman must decide whether it is better to demonstrate first or to visit, whether to cold call from canvass or to gather the basic information independently and telephone for an appointment.

After he has been selling the product successfully for awhile, the balance of calls for each customer category will become second nature to him.

The harder you sell, the heavier the whip you have to use to beat your own back. The more new calls you make, the more follow-up calls you have to make. The more orders you take, the more predelivery work you have to do and the more customers you have to service. The only way to keep on top is by planning.

On the other hand, the more calls the salesman makes, the more orders he will take. The more orders he takes, the more experience he gains. The more experience he gains, the better his rate of converting prospects to orders and the shorter his sales cycle.

Control procedures and documentation

A good salesman should use pen and paper in his planning. If he is not writing down the information, his is not planning—and, worse, he is not remembering all the things he should be doing.

If he is writing down the information, there is no reason why the salesman should not show it to his field sales manager and discuss it with him. The manager should be there as part of the same selling team. His task should be to help the salesman in achieving their correlated targets, rather than to sit in judgment over him.

The field sales manager should not require any further information than that which the salesman requires to plan and run his territory properly. Additional demands for information can be made only at the risk of diverting the salesman from his primary purpose, which is to sell.

It is vital that a salesman see his primary role as producing orders, and that this be the basic criterion on which his performance is judged. Once he is given the chance to do otherwise, he will find every excuse he can to avoid the continuing strain of face-to-face selling.

With few exceptions, numbers alone should be sufficient on the salesman's returns. If the sales manager requires detailed written reports of calls made, it suggests that he is reluctant to delegate full responsibility for the territory to the salesman and is prepared to assume some part of this responsibility himself.

The salesman spends 90 percent of his time alone in his territory. He can work effectively only if he is motivated to plan the optimum use of his time. This involves his having the responsibility for achieving targets, the authority to deal directly with the company's customers, and the financial incentives to encourage success. By usurping these functions the field sales manager breaks a basic bond and throws away the only hope he has that the salesman will work effectively on his own.

The salesman's field returns cannot take the place of discussion between the salesman and his manager. Instead, they should provide the basis for this discussion and guide the manager's efforts to help the salesman reidentify his planning function and check the relevance of his figures.

The sales manager's task in motivating his salesmen is primarily a selling task. As in any selling task, the technique he uses should be a questioning technique: questions beginning HOW, WHY, WHEN, WHERE, WHAT, WHO. These are open questions that bring a qualifying response. In effect, they leave the salesman with the feeling that it is his opinion that is being sought. In reality, they give the manager the opportunity to make his views a part of the salesman's thinking.

The planning control ratios that the salesman should concern himself with are *orders to hot prospect, new calls to total calls,* and *key calls to total calls.*

Orders to hot prospects

A hot prospect is a prospective customer from whom the order would already have been taken except for some special reason, such as the end of a financial period or a pending board decision.

There is obviously a direct relationship between the number of names on the hot prospect list and the rate of signing orders. It might be found in the capital goods industry, for example, that thirty good names on the hot prospect list will lead to an order rate of one a week. This order could come directly from the hot prospect list itself or from the salesman's efforts to build that list.

If the sales target in this instance is one order a week, the primary control requirement should be a hot prospect list of thirty names. Then, if the list of thirty names can be achieved, the likelihood is that the sales target will also be achieved.

Once the ratio of orders to hot prospects has been established, the salesman's job is first to build the list to the appropriate number and then to continue to replace all losses from the list with hot prospects of equal quality. Obviously, if he is allowed to fool himself about the quality of his hot prospects, he will fool himself and his manager about the number and size of his future orders.

New calls to total calls

Total calls are total calls made in a week. New calls are calls to prospective and existing customers *where new business is discussed for the first time.* This is an important definition.

Obviously, new business comes from new calls. Just as obviously, new calls not made today will result in new business not concluded tomorrow.

Going back to the example of the capital goods industry with an order-to-hot-prospect ratio of 1:30, let us say that to take the one order a week, the salesman loses three other names from his hot prospect list, leaving four names to be replaced. These will be replaced from his good prospect list (prospects who are definitely interested but with whom the sales negotiation is not complete) and from his new calls. If his good prospect list provides two hot prospects a week (and in turn loses two other names), he will have to find two more hot prospects from among his new calls. Thus he may have to make ten new calls a week to find four new good prospects and two new hot prospects. The call planning requirement, therefore, becomes ten new calls a week.

Follow-up calls, customer calls, and service calls will make up the rest of the calls for the week.

Key calls to total calls

In selling any type of product, there is usually one category of call that has to be made before the sale can be completed. This is the key call in the sale.

For capital goods the key call could be the demonstration, for technical equipment it could be the quotation, and for consumer products it could be a call related to a new promotion.

Activity in the key call area gives a good idea of business that will be achieved in the future. Activity that is required in these areas will directly influence the level of business that is achieved in the future. The capital goods salesman might therefore plan to make eight demonstrations a week out of a total of twenty-five calls (ratio = 8:25).

The danger in this is that selling itself can become a secondary task to setting demonstrations, writing quotations, and making special promotion calls. The secondary ratios of orders to demonstrations, orders to quotations, and orders to special promotion calls, therefore, must also be closely watched to ensure that activity in the key call area is effective.

Control documentation

Control documentation is necessary to monitor field sales activity. The salesman should be required to complete a *hot prospect list* once a month or once a week as a basis for discussion with his sales manager. In this discussion, the sales manager will be concerned with the quality of prospects and the mix of products.

In this instance, it has been assumed that the demonstration and the quotation are key calls in the sale. The significant column is the *date of order*—the date when the order will be placed. Unless this can be completed, it is hard to say that the prospect is *hot*.

HOT PROSPECT LIST

Salesman's name   Date

Company name & address	Product	Date of demon- stration	Date of quote	Date of order	Comments

In completing the form, it is worthwhile to fix the period when the order is expected at, say, three months and to show the orders expected in the first month followed by orders expected in the subsequent two months.

The salesman might prepare a similar list of his good prospects, using the *comments* column to show the action he intends to take next with each of them.

The *client contact report* shows the salesman how he has worked his week. This is important, as work completed now will result in orders taken in the future. Any imbalance in the relationship between calls can be noted immediately, and corrective action can be taken before the order rate is adversely affected. The report also shows the salesman that he is in fact working to his territory plan.

In terms of definition:

— A *canvass call* is a *cold call* to a prospective customer where the salesman has failed to get through to the *decision maker*. However, he has taken a name and telephone number and will probably telephone for an appointment later.

— A *new call* is a call in which new business is discussed with a new prospect or an existing customer *for the first time only*.

CLIENT CONTACT REPORT						
Name Branch Period No.						
Territory Date Week No.						
Category of call	Mon	Tues	Wed	Thurs	Fri	Total
1. TOTAL CALLS						
Canvass calls						
New calls						
Follow-up calls						
User calls						
Technical calls						
2. Demonstrations held						
3. Demonstrations arranged						
4. Quotations						
5. Orders						

— A *follow-up* call is a second or subsequent call to a new prospect.
— A *user call* is a follow-up call to an existing customer to discuss new or increased business.
— A *technical call* is a call to a customer to handle a problem or question.

These calls add up to make total calls. The format again assumes that demonstrations and quotations are *key calls* in the sale. By comparison with the previous weeks, the sales manager must ensure that demonstrations arranged result in demonstrations held and that demonstrations and quotations are converted into orders.

Initially, to be sure that the salesman really does understand the meaning of the call categories, or again if he is selling below quota, it might be necessary to require him to report his calls in greater detail. The *daily call sheet* would meet this requirement.

Ideally he should complete *purpose of call* before the call is made so that he learns to clarify his call objectives. However, the daily call sheet should really be used only in the short term. In the longer term it tends to be demotivating—it is a hard way to work a salesman

In addition to these lists, the salesman will also need a *forward plan* and some form of *customer record system*.

The forward plan needs to be no more than a diary. It is essential that sales management ensure that the salesmen are making firm future

DAILY CALL SHEET				
Salesman		Territory		
Date	Name & address customer/prospect	Purpose of call	Result of call	Orders taken, product & quantity

appointments for new, follow-up, and user calls so that they do not allow themselves to drift. The forward plan is also important so that management can discuss with the salesman his territory planning in terms of geographical coverage, coverage of the different categories of customer, and coverage of the different categories of customer by ordering date (for example, some local authorities may set their budgets early in April each year).

Most consumer product salesmen use customer record cards as a basis for planning their travel, and here a suitable system must be created and properly maintained. Other types of salesmen use notebooks or a variety of other recording systems. There is also a temptation among many companies to expand this system to cover customer information retrieval. However, although this can be desirable, it must be closely monitored to make sure that it is accurate and that it does not interfere with the primary selling activity.

3 Identifying the Customer

What are the markets for the product?

For a great many new products, development tends to concentrate on design and production specifications. Inevitably there is a customer category in mind, and advice is usually sought from the marketplace. Too often, however, this advice is given with no commitment to order and, too frequently, it is later found to have been worthless.

Experience shows that the markets that turn profitable for new products are often considerably different from the ones the innovator had in mind. For example, the range of industries that will be interested in the product may be known, but not specifically how the industries themselves will use it. It is only when a particular customer has spent x dollars to use the product to meet a precise need that the salesman can be sure that this particular market exists for his product.

The lessons in this are twofold. First, the wider the range of markets the product will fit, the more likely it is to succeed; the smaller the potential market area, the more important it is to obtain commitment to purchase at the design stage. Second, it is only *good selling* that will challenge traditional methods to establish new markets for the new product.

The good salesman will always thoroughly explore potential outlets for his product and identify the new arguments that will place his products in these outlets.

Consider a truck-washing-machine salesman. He might begin with food companies that have fleets of slab-sided delivery trucks that wash well and, because of their purpose, must be kept clean.

He might then move to fleet operators of other types of vehicles, beginning perhaps with tanker operators, not because their requirement for cleanliness is so high, but because the problems of washing are so much greater in terms of time and money.

He might then search out the other industries with washing problems that could be solved by his product, such as the freight cars of the railway industry or the containers of the shipping industry.

Meanwhile his company will be looking for complementary products that will expand the range he has to offer, and will modify existing equipment to expand the range of industries he can approach.

Each purpose for which the customer uses a product, and each reason he uses it, will differentiate the market for the product. The salesman must understand these market subsections so that he can know the range of sales arguments available to him in approaching any one customer.

Similar companies in the same industrial category may use the identical product for the same purpose but for different reasons. One company may use the truck-washing machine because it gives a high standard of cleanliness, another because it allows a fast turnaround of vehicles. Their reasons depend on how they see their problems.

Again, similar companies in the same industrial category may use the identical product for a different purpose but for the same reasons. For example, one company may use a particular copying machine for general copying because it copies onto ordinary paper. Another company may use the same machine to copy invoices as part of an accounting procedure for the same reason.

Once you have discovered the various markets to sell to, finding the individual companies is relatively simple.

As companies in a similar industry tend to be located together geographically, the types of customers you have will tend to be determined by your sales territory. A first job, then, is to determine and understand the market characteristics of the territory.

Customer lists are important both in maximizing repeat business and in getting the sale before your competition does. A comparison of existing customers and their ordering rates can reveal differences in the ordering potential between them. You must make it your job to know the reasons for these differences.

Customers are only too happy to tell you the names of their business friends who could use your product. Make sure you ask them. Having made the decision to use your products, they will support their decision in front of their friends in other companies. Be careful, however, of the name of the person they give you to contact. He may not be the decision maker although he may hold a similar position. Each company differs in the responsibility it gives to employees, and you could end up trying to sell to the wrong man. It is a good introduction to say, for example:

"Your friend Mr. Maycock suggested I call you."

Existing customers can come up with some pretty good ideas on who may be able to use your products. They can also have a good feeling for possible new applications for your product. Many times, of course, they can be just plain wrong.

Directories are another source of information. The better they are, the better they categorize the prospect.

There are also professional and trade lists, journals, and notices of meetings. If you can determine the business characteristic of an important group of customers, it is not difficult to find others in a similar line of business.

Government papers and publications usually include names and positions; and it can be a good idea to note committee chairmen.

Visible advertising is found on the sides of trucks, on television, and in the press. Trucks must carry telephone numbers or addresses. Advertising in the media may give you news of a campaign that might be important to you.

Local and national newspaper reports often precede the expansion of a company into your area, and usually mean that it is a good time to contact them for business. They will need equipment and products for their new premises.

Canvass calling or cold canvassing covers the ground thoroughly and has the additional advantage that you can see and judge the premises. The confidence of that knowledge may be important in future contacts. You also have an open hand to go away, go in for the name, or go in for the first call.

Good canvassing can produce up to twenty-five good names a day. Good canvassing is as good as the name you obtain. Cold calling from a canvass call again depends on the person you can see. It saves a cold telephone call and the time that takes. The question becomes whether you are better at cold calling or telephoning.

In canvassing, while you are getting a prospective customer's name, write down his telephone number as well. It is a small point, but you might spend hours searching for a telephone number when, with forethought, you could have acquired it in seconds.

Which customers should I sell to now?

The first customer to sell to is the one who will place his order now. If you do not sell to him, your competitors will.

The criterion is always to make the call to the customer who is about to make an inquiry. If you can do this, you will reduce the number of inquiries your competitors receive. This is another instance where sales *brain* will complement sales *brawn*. So sit down and think about it. Work it out.

— Which companies in which industries have recently changed their methods and will now need your product? Hit *them* first.
— Which companies have just moved into new premises and will be placing orders to reestablish their business? Hit *them* first.
— Who in your company has made a really innovative sale to place your product in an entirely new end use? Hit *similar* companies first.
— Are there any interesting companies just around the corner? If there are, call *them* today.
— What is the end use market that would be worth a fortune to you if you could penetrate it with a first sale? Hit the most *likely* candidate in that market today.
— Which companies in the market for your product have the least time-consuming buying procedure? Hit *them* first.

Otherwise, the calls you must make are the calls required by your territory plan. These again are the calls that will give you coverage by geographical area, by category of customer, and by category of customer by ordering date. Blend your calls in these three planning zones to give yourself maximum time utilization.

Time is the expensive scarcity in selling. Pattern your calls to get maximum customer buying response per unit of selling time.

Call the prospective customer next door today and not tomorrow. Work your territory by areas so that you spend the minimum time between calls. Cold call between fixed appointments. Write your quotations, letters, and sales reports outside selling time.

Decide which call path is the quickest way to the order. Should you cold call first, or telephone for an appointment, or go immediately to a demonstration, or mailshot?

Make all your telephone calls for the week together at the same time, say one half morning a week. Similarly, make all your demonstrations together, say on Friday of each week.

Don't go into your office in the morning. There is bound to be something to do there and you will lose the best selling time in the day. Have your customers leave messages.

Call for new and increased business and fit the other calls in as soon as you can. Orient your call pattern to gain orders, and give these calls priority.

Finally, don't waste your time on long shots. Remember, probabilities multiply rather than average. If, for example, there are three steps in achieving a sale and there is a 70 percent probability or chance that you will achieve each step, the overall probability of achieving the sale is not 70 percent, it is below 35 percent ($70\% \times 70\% \times 70\%$). So any situation where the overall probabilities are less than 50 percent is definitely a long shot. There must be a better call to make first.

Which man should I see?

The man to see is the man who makes the decision and can authorize the placing of the order for your product. How to get to him is a basic selling problem, but get to him you must.

The salesman must have the ability to identify his decision maker. However good he is in his presentation, no amount of selling will sell to the wrong man. You can talk your heart and soul away; but if you are not talking to the right man, you are not going to sell.

An early question in any presentation must determine whether you are talking to the right man (see the section "Questioning Techniques for Control and Information" in Chapter 5). For example:

"What are your responsibilities?" (*Direct open question*)

"Are you the man who makes the decision in this area?" (*Direct leading question*)

"How is the decision made in your company?" (*Indirect open question*)

"If I can satisfy you that my product meets the needs of your company, will you place the order for it?" (*Indirect leading question)*

You are talking to the wrong man if he has to go to another man for the final decision. The other man is the right man for you.

The rationale for this is that, although the sales argument is logical, the decision to make a decision is emotional. While you may be able to transmit the logical argument through a third party, it is unlikely that you will have the same success with the emotional factors.

Generally it is pointless to proceed with the sale if you find yourself with the wrong man. Usually it is better to break off the meeting diplomatically and to rearrange the appointment for a later date with the right man.

It is easier to break off a meeting diplomatically in the first instance than to go over the head of the wrong man later when you find that this is the only way you will win the decision.

The rule of thumb is to go high. You can always go down an organization but you cannot always go up.

It is therefore best to start with the president, of chief executive officer. If he delegates you to somebody else, ask him if the man he is sending you to can make the decision on his own. If he can't, point out that you would find it a real advantage to deal directly with the decision maker.

In a very large organization, it is unlikely that the president will make your particular decision. It might then be a department head.

You will learn to identify the decision maker for the particular product you are carrying. He is unlikely to have the same title in every firm. Companies differ in the responsibility they allow their employees.

It is almost standard throughout industry, however, that employees want to improve their status by taking responsibility for decisions for which they have no authority. So be careful not to be caught by the man who *says* he has the power to make the decision, but doesn't.

The buyer is usually not the right man except where the product involves routine reordering. Otherwise the buyer deals with the mechanics of ordering.

If your product involves a change in present company policy in any way, then you must go to the man who can institute policy change. He is usually an executive officer.

If you have strong product advantages to offer and the man who should see you will not see you to discuss your case, you have every right to go to his boss. You cannot lose an order you have not got; and that man should be doing his job properly.

The technique for finding the right man is to ask the right questions. Normally you will be questioning the receptionist or a secretary but, if you are selling to factories, you might find it more profitable to question production staff you meet in the yard. This approach can also help you fill other information gaps on, for example, existing suppliers and operating methods.

The way you ask the questions will influence the ease or unease you cause by your questioning and therefore your chances of obtaining all the information you want.

Keep firmly in your mind as you ask your questions that you are employed at the same level as the man you are seeking to meet and not at the level of the person you are questioning. If you can do this, you will go a long way in maintaining control of the dialog.

The real skill in this questioning technique is to hold the initiative. This means asking questions that require answers, rather than putting yourself in a position where you must answer questions.

Let us go back to the salesman who is selling sophisticated truck-washing equipment, this time to the transport section of a large industrial company. The transport manager is unlikely to be the right man. His job is to keep the trucks on the road. The top man is too far away from the problem. The chances are that he has placed control of this section in the hands of one of his fellow officers. The salesman's questions to the receptionist might therefore develop along this line:

S. You have a transport manager?
R. Yes.
S. Do you also have a traffic manager in charge of the movement of goods?
R. Yes.
S. Who is the man they both report to, the transport controller?
R. Mr. Chadwick.
S. Is he a director?
R. Yes.

Now that you have the information, you must decide immediately whether to leave or to ask for the cold call appointment. You must determine your objective at once and act quickly.

The more questions you ask now, the more chance you have of getting a difficult question thrown back at you. Similarly, the more questions you ask now, the less likelihood you have of achieving the cold call appointment or even getting through on the telephone at a later date. By going too far, all you are doing is winning yourself a place in their rogues' gallery.

The initiative in this questioning technique is achieved through surprise. The unexpected happened when you walked through the door and started asking questions. So don't throw away your best chance and allow answers to be qualified—don't begin by saying who you are and whom you represent. Unbalance the person with your questions and have her searching for the answers rather than the reasons why you are asking them. Keep your call card in your pocket.

Whatever you do, don't tell your story to the receptionist or the secretary on your way to your decision maker—not even if she smiles at you. Don't tell her why you want to talk to the decision maker, and don't let her persuade you to. That is your concern, not hers. Her job is to give you the name of the man to see and to put you through. That is another rule in selling: *The more people you tell your story to, the less chance you have of making the sale.* You will probably not even get through.

Never rely on the staff's being reasonable and helpful at this stage of the sale. Nine times out of ten they will try to reduce you to their level and exercise decision making over you. If you let them do this, you will lose their respect and probably your objective.

Do not accept freely anyone's advice on whom you should see. Keep your objective clearly in your mind. Ask the right questions, and then you will know you have the right answers.

Do not ask for any favors. The employees are just not going to give them to you. They owe you nothing. They are much more likely to favor the people they are working for and to whom they owe their jobs. In their eyes, that usually means keeping you out.

So speak with authority. Sound important and the receptionist may not chance a question. Sound unimportant and she will try to break you. If you are asked why you want to speak to the decision maker, reply with a question:

"Is he in?"

That will return the initiative to you.

If your argument is that it's important to establish good relationships with the staff in order to sell, then the counterargument is that you should establish these relationships after you have made contact with the decision maker. Otherwise, your attempts at being liked will be interpreted as weakness and you will be put down. Anyway, in business, respect is a better asset than being liked.

One sure way to establish a bad relationship is to ask for advice from a receptionist or secretary and then to disregard it.

If you have the company name, the telephone is a good way to obtain the contact name. You can prepare your questions beforehand. If you want the chief executive officer, "Who is the head man?" is the best question.

"Put me through to him" is the dangerous following instruction. By association, it can bring out a "Why?" and it is often better to put the telephone down and place a call to the name the next day. On the other hand, you cannot spend your life trying to get through to one prospective customer, and telephone calls cost money. It is then a question of judgment.

S. Is this Collins and Company?
R. Yes.
S. Good morning. Who is the head man there?
R. Mr. Chadwick.
S. Is he the president?
R. Yes.
S. My name is Lund. Put me through to him, please.
R. What do you want to speak to him about?
S. Is he in?

Cold calling produces the company name; and while you are there, you can try for the order. As you are looking for quick decisions, you would cold call only those companies with a short sales cycle. As in telephoning, success depends on being brief, direct, and forceful.

Mailshots can dilute the impact of any further presentation. On the other hand, they give a return of the 4 percent who are definitely interested. You can then telephone those who reply, and you have the right to speak to them because they asked you to call. The one big snag is that the person who replied does not have the power of decision but did have the time to answer your letter.

As far as letters are concerned, a salesman is kidding himself if he thinks he can get an appointment with the right man, or even find out his name, just by writing a letter. Worse, he is wasting his own time and his company's money.

The human motivational factors

The basis of any sales argument must be logic. If the proposition just does not make sense, the customer is not going to buy. Or, if he does, he is going to regret it, and the salesman is going to run into trouble.

The decision to make a decision, however, is emotional. Before he can buy, the customer must overcome an inherent reluctance to make a decision at all. This reluctance is natural because in business the decision is likely to cost money, and because the decision in one area precludes the choice of an alternative decision in that area. The salesman who can sell is the salesman who can put forward his proposition with a strong logical and emotional appeal for a decision.

An understanding of *human motivations* also helps the salesman in his personal relationship with the customer. If he can show an implicit understanding of his customer, the salesman is more likely to win his appreciation and confidence and reduce his hesitancy in making a decision.

If the salesman, on the other hand, appears *too* involved with matters of personal concern to his customer, he is equally likely to lose his confidence and his order. As in most things, the application is as important as the rule.

The customer, in buying a product, seeks to satisfy both personal and operational requirements. The personal or *primary* requirements are those factors in his inherent psychology that influence his personal and individual actions. The operational or *secondary* requirements are his business needs for a product that performs in a particular area.

A product that is bought for use in production, for resale, or for use in conjunction with other goods is a good example of a product whose secondary requirements are more important than the primary. Here the customer is mainly concerned with such factors as price, quality, availability, service, technical support, and specifications.

However, even in these instances—in fact, whenever he has a choice of companies in placing his order—the customer will still try to choose the salesman who has come nearest to satisfying his primary requirements.

Primary physiological needs are unlikely to be met frequently in selling. However, where there is a basic requirement for a minimum of warmth, lighting, or water, the matter is usually urgent and the customer will seek to satisfy his needs immediately, up to a minimum level, without considering his other primary needs. These are the easiest sales to make. Above this minimum level, the other primary needs become important.

Stressing the reward of more money is not good motivation. People tend to take the public attitude that money is bad, but the things it buys are all right. The good salesman will therefore either stress the things that money will buy or acknowledge the financial advantages only enough to place them in the customer's mind before laying emphasis on the other benefits.

The thesaurus of the primary needs that are important in selling is as follows.

Success: This includes the need for power, influence, status, position, money as applause, not falling behind, having the latest.

Esteem: This includes the need for being loved or liked, loving or liking, being attractive, being manly or feminine.

Permanence: This includes physical health and a desire for immortality; also the power and status that ensure survival.

Possession: This includes the desire for ownership, owning a successful company, having the things that are worth having.

Comfort: This includes the need for money for what it will buy, the ability to relax, the desire to avoid problems or responsibility.

Security: This includes the need for freedom from pain, worry, and fear, which can be achieved through position and status. Money is important in continuity rather than in quantity.

Each individual is made up of a blend of these factors. The blend varies from person to person, and varies within each person in relation to his particular social function, say as a businessman or as a family man.

Each individual has an ideal view of himself (his ego ideal), and this view determines and is determined by the factors that motivate him. The salesman achieves a greater personal rapport with the customer by recognizing these psychological requirements and appealing to them in his presentation.

The process for discovering the factors that motivate a person is:

— observing his physical aspect, how he dresses, the car he drives, the office he sits in, the way he lives
— listening to the way he expresses himself and the particular values he places on the subjects he discusses
— asking questions that develop the personal reasons for what he has done and what he intends to do
— deciding from this analysis the balance of psychological re-requirements he is seeking to satisfy

When properly chosen, the words success, esteem, permanence, possession, comfort, and security (and their synonyms) become important in selling. The salesman fits them into his presentation, particularly during benefit selling, as he points out the real advantages his product will bring to the customer.

In his presentation, therefore, the salesman probes the customer's primary and secondary motivations, basing his appeals on his own knowledge of the industry and the company's particular problems, and on his assessment of the individual he is dealing with.

The sales technique here is to make an indisputable statement in the area of the customer's motivation and then to commit him to an explicit statement of his attitude by following the statement with a question. For example:

Primary motivations

Success: "As you have said, it doesn't take a great deal of vision or analysis to see that this product is important to your company. What do you think your problems will be in getting a decision through the Board, and what would you like me to do to help you?"

Esteem: "It's an effective piece of equipment and your staff will be grateful to lose the drudgery of the existing methods. What do you think it is going to mean to them?"

Permanence:	"I'm sure you would agree that in your industry the profit goes to the company that stays in the forefront with the right new products and systems. What was the last innovation you made and what benefits did it bring your company?"
Possession:	*either* "A company as big and important as yours really cannot afford to do without a product like this. What would happen if you suddenly had to reduce deliveries to your ten largest customers?"
	or "Perhaps you are not yet big enough for equipment offering production figures like these. What expansion programs do you have in mind?"
Comfort:	"Believe me, it is going to make life much easier for you. For one thing, you are not going to have your boss breathing down your neck every time your present system goes wrong. How often does this happen?
Security:	"Even when your system is working well, it must sometimes worry you that it is going to collapse again and cause costly disruption to your production lines. What happened last time it broke down?"

Secondary motivations

"There is no question that, when you use our product, it is going to run just as well through your equipment and produce the type of job you are looking for. The greatest advantage you will find is in the purchase money saved. What other advantages do you think it will bring you?"

"I don't think there's any doubt that you'll make more money with this product range, although I know that for a shop with your turnover, a few pennies here or there are not going to make a great deal of difference. What additional profit do you in fact think it will give you?"

In addition to the needs expressed above, the customer also has a primary need for justice and fair treatment. This requires that the salesman treat him honestly, particularly in matters of price and the qualities he attributes to his product. If the customer loses faith in the salesman, psychologically he will find it difficult to do business with him, even if the salesman ultimately offers to remedy the area of dispute. This is the practical reason why there can be no place in selling for lying or misrepresentation. Gain achieved through deceit can only be short-lived.

4 Opening the Interview

Setting the objective

Sales objectives fall into two distinct categories: *call objectives* and *planning objectives.*

Call objectives are the agreements the salesman seeks to obtain from the customer so that he can ultimately achieve his primary objective, which is to take the order now. By definition, therefore, call objectives advance the relationship between salesman and customer.

Planning objectives are the actual categories of calls the salesman must make to advance his customer to the ordering point and to work his territory according to plan.

The salesman's primary objective in any call is to sell his products or to sell more of his products. This objective forms the basis of his relationship with the customer.

The salesman's whole approach to his customer should be determined by his primary objective to take the order now. He should do everything that is necessary to achieve this objective, and nothing that is not necessary to achieve it.

If the salesman fails to achieve his primary objective, he should try to settle for secondary objectives on a descending scale:

- To persuade the customer to agree to place his order next week.
- To persuade the customer to place his order subject to quotation.
- To persuade the customer to agree to a demonstration.

The only way to achieve an objective is to obtain the customer's agreement to the objective. This requires that the salesman ask the customer if he agrees to the objective (the *close*), and that the customer say yes he does agree to the objective.

Whether you are selling capital equipment or the good name of a business school, unless you actually ask for agreement to the objective and the customer actually says yes, you cannot say you have achieved your objective. It is often easier to avoid the apparent embarrassment of asking for the decision, and the result then is that the customer feels no greater commitment to your objective than he did the moment you walked in the door.

Without specific agreement to an objective, the call is a waste of time, energy, and money.

As a rule of thumb, the salesman should try to close his primary objective each time he calls in person on his customer. There is no need to feel embarrassed. The customer knows that is why you are there. Usually he prefers dealing with someone who is straightforward to dealing with someone who tries to dodge the issue.

Rationalizing your action by saying that the customer is probably happier with you because you did not ask for a decision is just nonsense. The only reason he saw you was that he has a problem in your area. If you walk out without any decision, he will still have the same problem and has gained nothing from the time he spent with you.

Again, unless you ask for a decision, you do not give the customer the chance to make clear in his own mind the real requirements he will want to satisfy in making his decision. Similarly, unless he is able to give expression to his objections to the decision, neither you nor he will ever know whether they are valid.

Remember, you are the expert in the area of discussion. Let your customer benefit from your expertise—develop the case for your product fully.

The primary objective for any call, then, is to take the order, and this objective must ultimately be *closed* if the sale is to be made. However, the salesman will also have to decide on the categories of calls he must make to advance the customer to a point where he is able to make his decision; and each of these calls, in turn, must have secondary objectives that must be *closed:* for example, a cold call to set an interview with the customer, a telephone call to arrange an appointment for demonstrating the product's capability, a site call to confirm site requirements and to close the order, and so on. Each separate call has a separate purpose and therefore a separate objective. Unless the salesman is able to achieve the customer's agreement on the necessary call objectives, he will never move to the point where he achieves the final decision.

The good salesman plans specific call objectives for every call he makes. These objectives are the purposes for which the call is made.

Unless the call has a purpose, there is nothing it can achieve. If the call has no purpose, it should not be made. Constantly calling back without defined call objectives annoys the customer and weakens the chance of future sales. This is the kind of *persistence* that gives the salesman a bad name.

It is a rule for any call in any circumstance: *Always have something to sell.*

The two objectives of every call are therefore to take the order if possible and, if not, to achieve the separate purpose of the call, which in turn is a step toward the order. In this way, the salesman will take the shortest route to each order. The number and types of calls he makes in a week over his whole territory can also be seen to have separate planning objectives that are important in achieving the annual sales objective or target.

Determining the objective you want to achieve is necessary before you can decide how you are going to achieve it. Certainly, you have to know how you are going to achieve it if you are going to go into a call fully prepared. If you are not fully prepared, you are likely to be caught off guard, and you then risk losing the order. What are some of these call and planning objectives?

Call type	Examples of possible call objectives
Canvass call	— To find potential customers for the product. — To obtain a contact name. — To cold call for an appointment with the contact name.
New call	— To show the new customer that his requirements are met by the product, and to take his order. — To establish his needs with him prior to inviting him to a demonstration.
Follow-up call	— To restress the benefits of the product to the customer, and to take his order.

— To carry in and explain a written quotation, and
to take his order.

— To commit him to making a decision, and to take
his order.

— To agree on a decision timetable, and to take his
order.

— To hear the Board's decision, and to take his order.

— To check site or stock details, and to take his order.

Telephone call — To set an appointment for a meeting or demonstration.

— To confirm the progress toward the decision.

— To confirm date and times of meetings.

— To provide information necessary for the evalua-
tion of your proposal but not critical to the
final decision.

Letters and — To confirm price, product information, product
quotations benefits, and the times and dates of meetings.

User calls — To resell the benefits of the product, and to confirm the continuing suitability of the product.

— To confirm product stocking or production characteristics, and to take repeat orders.

— To fight off competition, and to reaffirm the advantages of doing business together.

Technical calls — To make sure the staff is happy with the new
product.

— To persuade the customer to accept operator
training.

— To handle difficulties arising from breakdown, and
to indicate areas of better product operation.

— To commission equipment, and to sell the idea of a
maintenance contract.

Having set your call objective, be wary of the customer who tries to
persuade you to change it before you have achieved it. This often happens when the customer shows enthusiasm for the product and the
salesman is tempted to abandon one call objective for another. Too
often the salesman ends up with nothing, usually because he relin-
quished control of the interview to the customer.

So don't change one call objective for a higher one unless
very sure of yourself. Achieve one before going to the next. It
to take the order later than not at all. Similarly, allow your cu͟s   ..er
to persuade you to modify your call objective only when you are sure
it will not harm the achievement of your primary objective, which is to
take the order now.

If you are not sure how high you can go in your objectives, go high
and sell hard. You can always settle for a lesser objective, such as closing for the order and settling for the demonstration, or closing for two
orders and settling for one.

One way to make sure you establish and sell into call objectives is to
identify them for your customer early in your presentation. Even go a
step further and tell him how you intend to achieve them:

> "I've asked for this meeting with you because I'd like to per-
> suade you to buy one of our truck-washing machines. With
> your agreement, I'd like to spend this meeting identifying your
> requirements and briefly explaining to you what our equip-
> ment can do. Then, if you're interested in what I have to say,
> I'd like to invite you to a demonstration to show you the
> capability of our equipment. If you're satisfied with what you
> see, we can then discuss price and check siting, before arranging
> installation."

While it is dangerous to switch call objectives during a call, it may be
disastrous to offer different products as the solution to the same problem. The reason is easily understood. If you offer one product as a
solution to a customer's problem and, when this is rejected, offer another, the customer will assume, probably rightly, that you are more
interested in making a sale than in solving his problem. So make sure,
when you sell, that you obtain the information you need from the customer before you select the product and put forward your proposition.
Then, with the arguments in your favor, stick to your guns and sell hard.

The exception is when you sell different sizes of the same product.
The rule here, where there is no requirement for exact fit, is to sell the
size larger than the one you think the customer needs. You can always
settle for the smaller size. The customer's natural reluctance to spend
money will stop you from going too high; and, in the long run, the customer will be happier with the product he can grow into than with the
one that is already too small within a year of purchase.

So establish your objectives before you call, understand them, sell into them, and finally close them. And approach every sale as though it is the most difficult you have to make. Only then will you not take unnecessary risks.

Cold calling

Cold calling for an appointment has advantages in immediacy and in saving time.

You can cold call from a cold canvass for a name. You are there, so why not try to go through for an immediate appointment?

You can cold call between fixed appointments. This increases your chance of taking orders that day, and saves you from hanging around in coffee houses or bars.

You can cold call every day. Obviously, you can make many more calls in a day on a cold call basis when you are not constrained by fixed times. There are relatively few businessmen who are so busy that they have no time to see anybody; and, even if they are temporarily busy, you can always call back in an hour's time.

Cold calling also allows you to call on companies while you are passing through the territory. So many times, if you do not make the call then, you never will.

Cold calling can also be useful as a follow-up to precipitate the order. The prospective customer can put off the final appointment but, if you just park on his doorstep, there is a good chance that he will be persuaded to stop avoiding the decision.

Cold calling, however, does not take the place of telephoning for an appointment.

If you fail to get through on the cold call, there is little point in cold calling again and again, since they have now learned to keep you out. Too many salesmen do this, working hard making twenty calls in the day but achieving only one face-to-face contact. Once you have failed to reach the decision maker on a cold call, the time has come to use the telephone.

On the other hand, never set an appointment for a call by telephone when you can cold call.

Cold calling and cold canvassing give you a view of the outside and even the inside of the business. You learn quite a lot about your customer and can thereby present stronger arguments in setting the appointment for the interview. You can wander around a little and even speak to some of the employees.

You can thus gain confidence through being able to picture the company you are telephoning, and this is something you miss when you work from reference sources.

Whether you telephone or cold call, never try to get through to your contact by deception, by saying it is personal business or a private matter. He might understand this kind of approach from his child, but he will never accept it from a businessman, unless of course it *is* a private or personal matter.

Never use business cards on a cold call. They will very probably lose the appointment. Anyway, there is not so much information to be given to the receptionist that she cannot carry it in her head. There is no good business reason for using a card then. Give it instead to your contact at the interview.

Similarly, if the contact cannot see you, do not leave your card for him. In fact, leave as little information behind as you can. Then, perhaps, there will still be some element of surprise left when you telephone for an appointment later.

If the customer on a cold call says he will see you, don't sit forever in the reception room patiently waiting for something good to happen to you. Give him fifteen minutes and ask the receptionist to reconfirm the meeting. If you then do not see him in the next ten minutes, either go and make another call and return later, set a firm appointment with him through his secretary while you are there, or telephone the next day. Remember, your time is as valuable as his, and if you do not treat it so, he certainly will not. Neither will the receptionist.

It is not a disaster to fail to get through to the decision maker on a cold call. There is still more you can do later to set the appointment. It is a disaster, however, if you compromise and see the wrong man. The moment you do this you make the sale twice as difficult.

The general rule in cold calling is to give secretaries and receptionists as little information about yourself and your company as you can. If you can get away with giving only your name, you should. With the exception of your own and your company name, any other information you give should be as vague as possible.

Indeed, the more information you give to people on your way to the decision maker, the less likelihood you have of making the sale or even getting through to the interviews. The reason for this is quite simple.

The more information you give, the more opportunity you give with it for them to exercise control and decision over you.

Since getting through to the appointment is largely a control problem, you handle it the way you handle any control situation in selling. You ask questions that require answers, and this forestalls questions being asked of you.

Success in cold calling also depends on the words you use and the attitude you take. A few well-chosen words and a lot of confidence are important. Assume you have the right to be granted the interview; don't beg for it. Appear to be on the level of the man you want to see, not on the level of the receptionist.

Be strong; be positive; and keep a clear idea of your objective.

"Who is the head man?"

is inevitably the best question. Once you have his name, you have the chance to leave, or to say:

"Will you please ask him if I may speak to him for a few moments? My name is Lund."

To the question

"Which company do you represent?"

or

"Why do you want to see him?"

the answer is:

"Maycock Industries. Is he in?"

or

"Will you please ask him?

Now your problems begin to multiply. If you think the man will ask the receptionist why you want to speak to him, walk away—far enough so that the receptionist cannot speak to you while she is holding the telephone.

An alternative is to use the internal telephone yourself instead of trying to hold the conversation through a third party. If that is impossible, after you have fought with the receptionist for a few moments, use an important-sounding but vague word or phrase, the kind that will galvanize the decision maker into action and tell him nothing. But you are getting weaker. Not many such phrases exist and you run the risk of sounding corny. You'd better work out something good in advance, perhaps something to do with the *generic* description of the market you are in. For example, the exchange with your customer may take this course:

C. What do you want to see me about?

S. An investment program. May I come through to your office?

If you fail to see him right away, you can always try to set an appointment for the future, either directly on the internal telephone or with his secretary. She will want to know why you want to see him. She will have the time to work through your important-sounding phrase and telephone you back with the message: "Don't bother." That's the fun of being a salesman. Perhaps you would do better to avoid her and try to telephone for an appointment later. If you decide to see the secretary, but she insists on knowing the exact purpose of your visit, say:

"It is really rather complicated and that is what I want to speak to him about. Will he be free on Tuesday morning at 10:00 or Wednesday morning at 10:30?"

Try an *alternative close* to get her mind onto a choice of dates and away from her main question. Then, as she pries additional information out of you, answer with one- or two-word replies and follow them up with leading questions:

"Is he in?"

"When will he be free?"

"Would next week be more suitable?"

There is a very good chance that she will break before you do. But whatever you do, don't try to sell your product to her; and don't let her put you off to a man you know is not the decision maker.

If you manage to get an appointment during a cold call, remember to set the next appointment before you leave—that is, if you fail to take the order across the table.

Once again, if the right man is not in, telephone or call back another day. Seeing the wrong man is a sure way of losing the sale.

If you fail to set an appointment at a cold call, setting the appointment by telephone will be that much more difficult because you have lost some of the element of surprise—though you should try. Your last chance is a letter, which is just slightly better than useless. You must succeed with the cold call if that is your decision.

If you have little success cold calling, develop a good telephone technique and end your cold canvass the moment you have the contact's name. Concentrate your energies on the things you are good at doing.

Telephone technique

The telephone has many uses:

- Setting appointments for new, follow-up, user, and technical calls.
- Extending invitations to demonstrations, exhibitions, and conventions.
- Confirming dates and times of meetings.
- Canvassing for names.
- Seeking information about a company, a man, or a process that is indispensable to the sale.
- Following up the progress of a sale.
- Keeping in touch with existing customers and potential problems.

The telephone has many advantages. It can be used to cover a lot of customers and territory quickly. It is unexpected and sudden and gives you initial control. The customer cannot see you and must base his decision on what you say and the way you say it. It requires a quick decision from him when you have the advantage of preparing what you have to say carefully beforehand. You hold the choice of the subject under discussion because you can ask the first question. And you can withdraw quickly if you find you have the wrong man.

The disadvantage is that he can cut you off by simply replacing the receiver. You must create interest immediately and achieve your objective without hesitation. You have to pass through a switchboard operator and a secretary who may be under the impression that they are paid to keep you out.

Generally, you should not prearrange an appointment you can cold call. Fixed time appointments reduce your flexibility in selling, although they are important in providing a framework around which a day's calls are made.

You should prearrange your visit if it increases your chance of success, if it increases your effective selling time, if it does not increase the risk of refusal, and if it does not create additional sales resistance.

While you might be able to take repeat orders by telephone or letter, there is just about no chance that you will take a new order that way. So don't try it. Give as little information about yourself as you can in setting the appointment; and do your selling when you are in his office. You will need all your surprises then.

If your contact is not in, *do not* leave your company name and telephone number with his secretary or receptionist. Otherwise, when he comes in, he may decide he does not want what you're selling and that will be that. If you must leave something, leave your own name; but leave that only grudgingly. One way to avoid questions in this situation is to say "Thank you, I'll call back later" and put the telephone down—and say the same thing even if the question has been asked.

Always retain the initiative on the telephone. If the contact is not in, make sure you telephone back at a time when you know he will have returned. If he is in and asks you to telephone back another time, either try immediately to set a provisional appointment with him which it will then be his responsibility to break, or get him to specify a date and time when you can telephone back.

Never write a letter to seek an appointment unless the appointment is overseas. If you cannot say what you have to say on the telephone, you should not be selling. If your contact will not speak to you on the telephone, either telephone someone who is a little more important in the company or go and sell to another company.

Once you have set the appointment, reconfirm the details and say goodbye. If you stay on the telephone, the only thing you can do is lose the appointment.

The temptation to continue talking comes when the contact accepts your appointment enthusiastically. The release of pressure deludes you into thinking he really likes you. Off you go with your story and, before you know what has happened, you have given him a reason to change his mind.

If you give away too much information on the telephone, it is just likely that he will make his decision there and then. Now, how are you going to get in?

If he goes on asking for information, tell him that it is a little complicated and that you would prefer to discuss it when you see him.

Alternatively, tell him that the terms and physical conditions for using the product vary by user even in the same industry, and that you are arranging to meet him so that you can find out what his exact requirements are.

If he insists on the information over the telephone and tells you he will not see you under any circumstances, try again to set the appointment, tell him it is impossible to give him the information over the telephone, and politely say goodbye. You will have more chance to set the appointment on another day than to persuade him to change his mind once he has made a decision over the telephone.

When you speak to the receptionist over the telephone for the first time, do not tell her why you are telephoning. As in cold calling, every additional person you speak to weakens your sale. Put pressure on her to put you through. Do not seek her favor. The name of the person you wish to speak to and your name are all the information she requires to do her job properly.

> S. Mr. McDermott, please.
> R. Who is speaking?
> S. Lund. (*Slightly louder*)
> R. Which company are you, sir?
> S. Is he in?

Keep your objective in mind. Do not be sidetracked into talking with her. The more she persists in asking questions, the more you should imply that she is not acting within her responsibility. Put an edge on your voice. She is wasting your time with her questions. Insist that she put you through:

   S. Let me speak to him, please.
   R. May I know what company you represent?
   S. Put me through, please.

Intelligently. Not rudely. The second time will be easier. Just make sure there is a second time.

If the customer is overly defensive through his secretary, you can bet you are going to run into problems. He is either not at one with his job or not at one with himself. Be careful. Again, keep your talking to a minimum. Your statements should commit the secretary to putting you through. By the nature of the situation, she is asking the questions. Try to reverse this role by asking the questions yourself:

      S. May I speak to him?
  SEC. What do you want to speak to him about?
      S. Is he in?

Put pressure on her. Throw her off balance and bring control of the conversation into your own hands. Work on the assumption that these people are not reasonable. You are on the boss's level, not the secretary's. The moment she feels you are on her level, she will decide you should not be speaking with her boss, and you will be lost.

If the man you want to speak to is not in, telephone back. Do not speak to anyone else, do not try to arrange the appointment with his secretary unless he is expecting you, and do not leave your name. If he is on another line, wait for him or telephone back. Do not leave your number for him to telephone. Retain the initiative.

Whatever you do, do not get yourself into the situation where you are asked to send a brochure and to telephone later. Your time and your company's money are being wasted.

Similarly, don't shoot a brochure off in the mail to a man you are going to see. He may just telephone you back to say he knows everything he wants to know about your product and he will telephone you again when he is interested. Similarly, don't fire brochures at people who will not see you. If you must send them something, put their names on your mailshot list. Before you do that, however, you would probably do well to try to find a better contact.

Never, never use the telephone to sell the final objective, the order. You are not on the scene to get the signature. By the time you have taken the fastest taxi in the world, the customer will have changed his mind.

The telephone is ideal for follow-up. Put the customer on a decision timetable and follow up regularly on the telephone. Never telephone unless you have something interesting to ask or to offer. Otherwise you will be justifiably accused of pushing too hard.

Always telephone the customer the day after a meeting, or the day after he has received your letter or quotation, to thank him for his interest and to ask him if he has any fresh inquiries on his mind. It allows you to reestablish contact with him on the friendliest basis, and it brings your proposal forward for consideration. It also gives you the chance to make the next appointment if you have not already done so.

If your customer telephones you, make sure your secretary does not tell him you are "not available at the moment," or you are "at a conference." It sounds as though you are telling him to wait his turn in your already heavy schedule, and he just may feel that his time is more important than yours. It is better if your secretary gets his name and telephone number, and says, "I'm afraid he's out at the moment; may he phone you back?" Then make sure you do phone back within the day.

Telephone this week for appointments next week. Do not let the appointments get too far ahead, otherwise the customer will forget why you want to see him.

Every telephone call is a sale on its own. As with any sale, set your objective beforehand and try to close in the first, second, or most promising subsequent sentence.

Keep your original objective. To change objectives midway can be disastrous. Make up your mind what you want from the call and stick to it. Create the pattern of approach around it.

On the telephone, *particularly* on the telephone, he who hesitates is lost. Similarly, a wandering story gives evidence of a wandering mind.

If you feel after an unsuccessful telephone call that you could have advanced the objective, learn from your mistake and improve your technique.

Interest your customer. He has probably had a hundred calls before you telephoned. Make sure yours is the one with the difference. Do not get him on the line and launch off into an endless tirade. Get him asking questions. It is a fine rule in selling. Make the bait look interesting and the customer will snap at it. Once he has asked you about your product, he will not stop you when you begin telling him. Your problem will then be to tell him only enough to gain the appointment.

One way to excite interest is to sound like an interesting person. Even when you are feeling miserable, make sure you are physically smiling when you talk. It will be heard at the other end of the line. No one wants to talk to a miserable man, and your customer may just see you because you sound attractive.

Arrange to use other companies' and other people's names as references to help you set an appointment. A man is much more likely to see a salesman with whom he feels some connection than to see a complete stranger. Make that link for him.

The objective of your first telephone call is to set an appointment either for a meeting or for a demonstration.

You could make the demonstration your first face-to-face contact if you know the product will have to be demonstrated before it is bought. Then you will have to give the customer just enough information over the telephone to influence an affirmative answer without weakening your future presentation.

To set the demonstration, you will have to introduce your company. You have the choice of playing it as a big name he should have heard of, or as a new company with an exciting product to offer:

> "Mr. Chadwick. It's a beautiful day, isn't it? (*Small pause*) My name is Lund. I'm with Wash-Clean Truck Washing Machine Company. We have a new automatic truck-washing machine which will wash any of your vehicles clean in less than three minutes. We are holding a special demonstration on Wednesday at our premises just around the corner from you. I'd like you to come. Is 3:00 in the afternoon convenient for you, or is 3:30 more suitable?" (*Alternative close*)

Any questions he asks now can be answered with a statement answer followed by another question close. It is a good telephone technique. It keeps the pressure on and the call short. It keeps the customer on the defensive:

> C. Why would I want a new truck-washing machine?
> S. I know I can give you cleaner vehicles at a lower unit cost. Which time do you prefer, 3:00 or 3:30?

If he agrees to the appointment, you must in one brief statement give him a good reason to come to the demonstration site. He must be convinced that you have something to show him. Otherwise he will say yes on the telephone and break the appointment. You must leave the vital benefit firmly embedded in his head, and this without throwing the objective away by talking too much.

To set an appointment for a first meeting it is invariably better to be abrupt and to the point:

> "Mr. McDermott. Good morning. My name is Lund. I'd like to come and talk to you. Is Monday afternoon at 3:00 all right, or would Wednesday afternoon at 2:30 be better?"

Do not just give your name and sit back quietly waiting for the heavens to fall on you—for surely they will. State, then *close:*

> C. (*Looking through his diary*) Which company do you represent?
> S. Wash-Clean. If it suits you, Monday would be a better day for me.

The less you say the better:

> C. Why do you want to see me?
> S. Vehicle cleanliness. Is Monday afternoon at 3:00 or Wednesday afternoon at 2:30 more suitable?

State, then *close again.* And don't be delegated to someone else:

> C. Mr. Meadow is the man you should see.
> S. Is he the man who can authorize orders?

If the answer is no, you must insist on seeing the man who makes the decision. There is no alternative. You must press him and, if he will not see you, obtain some form of commitment from him:

> "If Mr. Meadow agrees that my product is worthwhile for your company, will you personally come to the demonstration?"

Commit him to action. And set the date for the demonstration if possible.

Another successful telephone technique is to build your case with confident question-statements that interest and involve. Your objective is to make arrangements for a demonstration and you have to give the customer an idea of your business.

You introduce yourself:

> S. Mr. Penguin? My name is Lund. You have a fleet of vehicles, don't you?
>
> C. Yes.
>
> S. How many do you have?
>
> C. Fifteen. (*A useful piece of information*)
>
> S. Well, you're obviously quite a large fleet owner.
>
> C. Yes, I am. (*And I'm proud when I say it.*)
>
> S. And like all large fleet owners (*all important men*) you have a difficult washing problem.
>
> C. Yes, I have. (*Following the previous yes*).

Now you are in a strong position for a statement-and-question close:

> "I can wash any one of your vehicles all over in less than three minutes for half your current cost. I'd like you to come to a demonstration I'm holding next Wednesday afternoon at Gower Bros. nearby. Will 3:00 to 3:30 be suitable for you?" (*Direct close*)

Or you can throw the grenade that looks like a ball:

> "We have a revolutionary vehicle-washing system. If I can solve your washing problem and save you half your current expenditure, would you order one of my machines?"

It is very strong because it is very reasonable and very direct. The use of the word *order* puts it right on the line. The customer will probably try to slip out from under:

> "I'd have to see it first."

You've achieved your demonstration objective. On rhe other hand, he might just say that he wants your product on the evidence provided by third parties, in which case you discuss it no further but set an appointment to meet with him at once to get his signature.

Seek commitment. It will draw out the company that is about to be merged and the man who is not in a position to sign. And it sets the scene for the next meeting.

The key to selling is commitment. It is no good to negotiate along the lines of your logic and expect an order at the end of it. The customer must agree to the logic of the sale first. Then you can commit him to action. Once he has committed himself to action, he is duty-bound—if only in his own mind—to keep to his commitments. Commitment helps him through his decision.

Whatever you do, stay away from price. Price can end the sale right there on the telephone. Keep it for your final meeting, when you will have had the chance to show him what the product will do for him. If you are pressed, answer in general terms: "It is inexpensive" (the word *cheap* suggests poor quality). Say that the payment scheme is a little too complicated to discuss on the telephone or that it depends on the product specifications most suitable for meeting his needs. Say anything, but do not give him the price.

And *close*. If you do not close, you will not sell. You cannot close the sale on the telephone, but you can close the objective of the call. If you do not close during the telephone call, you will never get to the next stage of the sale.

Creating interest

There are two problems in opening the interview. The first is to obtain an appointment with your decision maker in a place, such as his office, where it is possible for you to talk business with him. The second is to introduce your presentation in such a way that you are able to move easily to the next step in the sale, which is *getting information*.

To be sure of success in obtaining the appointment during a telephone or cold call, it is important to be able to establish immediate interest. The sales method here derives from two techniques:

> *Positive motivation*, to persuade the customer that his time would be well invested in seeing you.

Negative motivation, to create in the customer an awareness that his present system is causing needless loss or risk.

A worthwhile investment of the customer's time can be achieved by suggesting that you can solve a problem you know exists in his company or industry:

"I understand that, together with most other companies in your industry, you are having trouble finding an economic way to meet government regulations on vehicle cleanliness. I believe I can solve this problem for you. Would you give me five minutes of your time, say on Tuesday at 10:30 A.M., or would Wednesday at 2:30 P.M. be more suitable?" (*Alternative close*)

Alternatively, you can make a claim for your product that suggests an indisputable profit to the customer:

"We've just brought onto the market a revolutionary vehicle-washing system which will wash any of your vehicles, irrespective of size or shape, all over in less than three minutes, at a wash cost lower than your present method. May I come to your office to discuss it with you?" (*Direct close on a cold call*)

However, don't use three benefits if you can get away with one, because it weakens your future presentation. On the other hand, use enough to achieve the customer's agreement to the interview without becoming involved in a discussion.

You can make the customer aware of the needless loss or risk in his present system by suggesting to him that there are better, cheaper ways of doing things:

S. How much of your valuable time is written off making sure your vehicles are properly cleaned every day?
C. One hell of a lot. Why do you ask?

Obviously the two techniques for obtaining immediate interest are complementary and can be used together.

Introducing your presentation, once you are seated in the customer's office, is equally important. The first two minutes you spend there could be the last two. You have two minutes to get him interested enough to continue the conversation.

What you say now could well decide whether you make the sale or not. First impressions are important, and bad first impressions can be difficult to overcome, even later in the sale.

The first rule to get very firmly into your head before you begin your presentation is that you are there to solve the customer's problem and not just to tell him about your product.

Before you can hope to provide the solution, you must find out exactly what his problem is. Definition of the problem comes as the next step in the sale. Only after you have defined the problem should you give an explicit description of your product—as you show *how* your product satisfies his requirements.

Your first sentence, therefore, should introduce you:

> "My name is Philip Lund and I'm the southern area manager for the Wash-Clean Company." (*Hands over call card*)

The second sentence should say why you are there:

> "I see you have a good number of trucks in your yard and I'm interested in talking to you about the obvious problems you have keeping them clean."

The third sentence should be a question that checks that he is the decision maker in this area:

> "I understand that you're the transport manager. Are you personally responsible for all decisions affecting vehicle washing or are they normally put before the Board?"

The fourth sentence should then question his current situation:

> "How do you tackle your truck-washing problem at the moment?"

By the time he has answered this question, you should have a very clear idea of how you intend to proceed with the sale and the basis on which it will be made.

Make it a rule: *Always ask a question by the third sentence.* Remember, the customer prefers talking to listening.

At this stage you are only trying to make him interested enough in talking about his problems to move to the next step in the sale, which is to get the necessary basic information.

If he does not answer your question, sit there and look at him until he does. Don't start answering it for him. If he answers but answers briefly, ask him another question, and then another.

Questions beginning HOW, WHY, WHEN, WHERE, WHAT, and WHO will disclose his present situation, the problems he has, and his attitude to his problems. Once he starts answering questions freely, you are already moving to the next step in the sale.

If you are really stuck for an opening gambit, ask yourself what *you* would like to hear in his position. If the customer still does not start talking to you, ask him a conditional question (*trial close*):

> "*If I* could offer you a better vehicle-washing method at less than your current operating cost, *would you* at least be interested in talking about it?"

A reasonable man could not say no. If he does say no, you can only terminate the meeting and leave. The suspicion is that the man you have been talking to is not the decision maker. So when you're back in the territory, perhaps you should telephone his boss.

Most salesmen are not given two chances to sell. Make sure you give yourself the best chance of taking the order the first time around.

The physical conditions for the sale

It is always better to sell to a man while he is sitting down. Standing up, he can walk away from a decision. Sitting down, it is more difficult for him to escape.

If you try to develop your sales presentation at the initial interview while standing up, the customer is likely to walk you right out of the door.

However incidental the item you sell may seem to be, always treat the business you have to do as important to both you and your customer. If you treat it as important, you will be halfway to having your customer treat it as important too.

Remember also that whatever business your customer is in, he has something to sell too. So don't be embarrassed in selling your product.

If you meet him in the reception room, therefore, introduce yourself and suggest that you go to his office. Tell him you want to use a table, and just stand there and look at him until he takes you to his office.

There are too many interruptions and too many different things happening in reception rooms to allow the customer to give you the full attention you need. If you have managed to arrange the meeting in the first place, a short step will change the meeting place to one more suitable.

Similarly, if at a demonstration or site check you think the customer is ready to sign the order, end whatever you are doing and suggest that you go to his office to finalize the details. If you try for the signature with the customer standing, he may just feel he is being rushed and ask for more time to consider. In the security of his office, he will feel able to give his full consideration and therefore his signature.

In the initial stages of the sale, the psychological relationship between customer and salesman is competitive, with the salesman attacking and the customer defending. The salesman alters his position by taking the same side as the customer, seeking his opinion with questions, and concerning himself with the customer's problems.

This competitive relationship tends to be emphasized by the natural line of the customer's desk, the customer sitting on one side and the salesman on the other. The salesman should recognize this as a physical barrier in his negotiation and try to sit on the same side of the desk as the customer, or at least at the corner. One way to achieve this is to use visual aids that require the two people to sit alongside each other.

If the customer and the salesman enter a conference room together, the conference table might also serve as a physical barrier, and the salesman should endeavor to sit next to the customer rather than opposite him.

It is also undesirable during the sales negotiation for the customer or the salesman to be seen standing while the other is sitting. This tends to imply either a teacher (standing)/student relationship or a king (seated)/subject relationship, depending on the people involved. Doing the same thing, sitting or standing, maintains the neutral position. It is quite a good point to remember when you are stopped by a traffic cop!

On the other hand, movement gains attention. If at any stage you feel you are losing the customer's attention, it may be a good idea to leap to your feet and take a turn around the room; or, alternatively, you might bang the desk to emphasize a point.

Avoid interruptions. The sequence of events in a controlled sale creates a dynamic influence that will move the customer to a decision. Interruptions will break the concentration and reduce this influence, and therefore lessen your chances of making the sale.

The sequence in the sale also creates a mood in which the customer feels like buying. Again, interruptions will disturb this mood, and even though the customer might like to buy, he will reject the decision now so that he can consider it later when he feels he has more time.

If you are constantly faced with external interruptions in the customer's office that are likely to influence the final decision, it is better to leave your presentation incomplete while you still have something to say and reset the appointment again either at your premises or at a demonstration site, where there will be no interruptions.

If it looks as though you are going to be faced with constant interruptions either from the telephone or from secretaries, ask your customer if it is possible to have fifteen minutes of his uninterrupted time. Explain to him that the concepts involved are reasonably complicated, that it will be important for him to understand them, that you know he is a busy man, and that, if you can have those fifteen minutes, he will then be free to handle all his other problems afterwards.

If you have prearranged this appointment, you should expect your customer to give you his uninterrupted time. After all, interruptions are discourteous and he would not like it if the same happened to him in your office. So as soon as the interruptions become oppressive, look bored; the more you are interrupted, the more bored you should look. Sooner or later he will notice you and apologize. As soon as he does, smile, say "that's quite all right," and continue with your sale.

After an interruption, always resummarize to make sure that you are both back at the same point, and continue.

Mailshots

Mailshots skim the market. Generally they should be used where there is a requirement to skim customers from the top of the market.

Response to repeated mailshots to the same market tends to decline as the top segment of the market is progressively absorbed. As the response declines, the cost of each response, and therefore of each sale, increases. Once the cost of the mailshot exceeds the profit from the sales generated by it, the argument for maintaining the mailshot program must be supported by evidence other than financial, or it cannot be supported at all.

Direct selling through a sales force is best where it is necessary and economically viable to sell into a market in depth. The mailshot then should be absorbed as a part of the salesman's territory sales program.

The mailshot has certain great advantages in territory selling:

- It can be used selectively in specific markets.
- It can be used selectively in time to hit seasonal markets and budget dates.
- It can be used to spread news of a new product, process, or end use over a large market area quickly.
- It can cover market segments which the salesman must neglect in the short term, as a foil against the encroachment of competition.
- It can be used as an initial approach in slow-moving market segments where immediate reward is unlikely but where the long-term possibilities are good.
- It can be used as a follow-up for prospective customers who are fully aware of the product but who either have not said yes or have said no when they have a compelling purpose for the product.
- It can be operated by the salesman at arm's length, either through his sales office or an agency, without materially increasing his workload or reducing the selling time available to him.

The mailshot has two disadvantages, particularly in opening new business. It tells the prospective customer you are coming, so that you lose an important element of surprise; and it runs the risk of feeding him the reason to say no before you have had the chance to meet him.

The net advantages of the mailshot to the salesman are obvious; it should be part of his everyday artillery. The objective for his mailshot must always be to gain the appointment.

A mailshot to open new business is ideally used to identify the top percentage of *most interested* customers. Once you have broken into a new market segment, the potential of that market will grow as you increase the number of user-customers and, therefore, the fund from which you can draw third-party recommendations.

A good mailshot should produce a 4 percent return, that is, four replies in one hundred, out of which you should be able to take two orders. The returns are selective, because the respondent has already expressed an interest and therefore can be readily turned into a *hot* prospect.

On the other hand, the respondent may be a person who has the time to reply, rather than the decision maker to whom the mailshot was addressed. In this instance, it might be wiser to let the opportunity lapse and to make an appointment with the decision maker by telephone at a later date.

A mailshot can be made up from just about anything: publicity material, an advertisement, a news item about a new customer or a new application, a planned exhibition or demonstration. The rule is always: *Sell news.*

If you have anything with news content, it has mailshot potential. Copies of the material, with a covering letter, are fine, and a red pen can be used sparingly to emphasize a point.

Brochures should be used only after a great deal of thought. If you put too much information in the hands of the customer, he may just decide that there would be no purpose in meeting you. Special brochures, however, can be created for mailing.

Mailshot material should give the recipient the impression that he is the only one receiving that piece of mail. Mass editions only serve as a warning and largely end up in the wastebasket.

The mailshot letter should cover no more than one sheet. It should be simply written and carefully punctuated, and should consist of short sentences. It is better neatly typewritten and handsigned, but there are some machines that can do a comparable job. Duplicated letters are terrible—unless of course you are selling a duplicator!

Otherwise the letter should follow the rules governing sales letters. It should be constructed in four paragraphs.

The first paragraph should state the objective of the letter:

> "I am writing to invite you to a special meeting of insurance brokers at Universe Hall on Monday, March 12, at 11:30 A.M."

graph should show why the topic is relevant to the

> "At this meeting, we are giving details for the first time in this
> country of a new investment plan designed to provide young
> householders in their twenties and thirties with an unprecedented
> level of financial security."

The third paragraph should show why the topic is of particular interest
to the recipient:

> "We feel that it is particularly important that you come to this
> meeting because we believe that our new investment plan can
> potentially double the size of insurance business from these age
> groups over the next five years. Our estimates of the growth in
> this market during this period are attached."

The fourth paragraph should then restate the objective and indicate
the action you will take:

> "I hope therefore that you will be able to join us at Universe
> Hall on March 12, and I shall telephone you next Thursday to
> confirm your attendance at the meeting."

The mailshot must indicate the action you will take. It gives you the
reason to telephone and should be followed up within a few days of
sending. Only in exceptional circumstances, or when you know you
will get the reply you want, should you require action on the part of
the recipient.

Mailshots must be sent to decision makers by name. There is no
purpose in just launching a letter into a company. Letters should be
planned not to arrive on Mondays, Fridays, or weekends.

Mailshots should be sent out in batches at the rate that will permit
follow-up without disruption of normal call requirements. If you are
running a large and costly mailshot program, it is also a good idea to
confirm the cost effectiveness of the program by sample testing a number of different approaches and choosing the best one.

Mailshots may go out to any number of recipients, from one to a
million. They should be part of the salesman's daily experience.

Leads and inquiries

Getting leads and inquiries is not just a matter of luck. The *lucky* salesman is almost inevitably the one who works hardest. The number of leads and inquiries a salesman receives is closely related to his work effort.

The salesman can do a lot to encourage leads and inquries from his territory:

- He can give his territory wide call coverage, both geographically and in terms of categories of customer.
- He can operate a high new call rate.
- He can open negotiations for his product with new customers in new market segments.
- He can offer his existing customers viable new proposals that will increase the turnover of his product with them.
- He can maintain a high level of mailshot activity to open new markets, to follow up prospective customers, and to offer new applications to existing customers.
- He can increase the value of his existing customers by encouraging them to mention his company and his products to their business friends.
- He can maintain a high level of activity in new product promotions, demonstrations, and exhibitions.
- He can persuade his colleagues to feed him leads about their territories by offering to do the same for them about his territory.

Where the company is operating a sales force that sells direct to the customer, the advertising and public relations campaigns should emphasize the objective of returning specific inquiries rather than selling the product. The purpose in creating inquiries is to make the salesman's job of setting the appointment with high-potential customers easier. Once he has the appointment, he is in a position to sell his product at the interview.

A clear understanding of the *inquiry-creating* objective is particularly important for small companies with only limited funds to spend on sales promotion programs. These programs may include trade promotions, press editorials, and advertising. The inquiry return slip should provide the salesman with the name, address, and telephone number of the inquiring company and the contact's name and position.

Direct-mail programs should be undertaken only with the approval and field support of the salesman. Telephone calls within a day or two of the mailing will increase the rate of response.

As the effect of an inquiry is to create the opportunity for an appointment, all inquiries from his territory should be forwarded to the salesman for action as quickly as possible. It is for him to decide how the inquiry should be handled: whether to cold call or telephone for an appointment or to answer by letter. If he is wise, he will arrange to contact his office twice a day so that he can collect his inquiries while they are still *hot*.

Most unsolicited inquiries ask for specific product or price information. It is disastrous to give this information freely over the telephone, by letter, or by sales office staff. Where sales are completed only during face-to-face contact and the problem is in setting the appointment, the inquiry must be regarded as a means to that appointment. The sales office staff must therefore be trained to handle all telephone and letter inquiries in such a way that the initiative to set the appointment is still retained by the salesman.

It is similarly disastrous to answer an inquiry by mailing a brochure—or, worse, a price list. This may provide the customer with the answers he thinks he needs (*which could be the wrong ones*), and preclude the appointment.

Inquiries seldom ask the salesman to call. In fact, usually the salesman is specifically asked not to call. In most cases where there is a chance for new business, the salesman should find a way to make a physical appearance in front of his customer. Sales are made by the salesman showing the customer precisely how the purchase will benefit him and eliminating any misunderstanding, rather than by the customer instinctively doing what is best for himself on unqualified information. Generally speaking, it is impossible for the salesman to do this over the telephone or by letter.

It is poor judgment for the sales manager to sit in his office by the telephone and then sortie out into the sales territories in response to the best of the inquiries. If he wants to pick the fruits of territory selling, he should be prepared to accept his share of the drudgery. Conversely, if he expects his salesmen to accept the drudgery of territory selling, he must let them handle their own inquiries, which are the fruits of their labors. He would be a wiser man to pass the inquiry straight on to the salesman and wait to be invited to make the call.

On the other hand, as a salesman, you should feel embarrassed if a new unsolicited inquiry reaches you before you reach the customer. You should have been able to identify beforehand the customers who would be interested. What would have happened if the customer had sent that inquiry to one of your competitors; or, alternatively, if he was just too lazy to do anything and learned to live without your product?

5 Getting Information

Information as the basis for the sale

Having opened the interview, the salesman must next bring together the basic information the customer needs before an effective sales proposition can be made.

The reasons for this are obvious. The salesman has to decide whether the customer is in the market for one of his products, which product he should offer, and how he is going to present his sales argument.

At this stage in the sale, the salesman is still asking questions. He should not yet begin to talk about his product. Any question he receives in return from the customer should be answered briefly in general terms and countered with another question. This effectively keeps the right to question and the control of the questions in the salesman's hands.

The basis for the salesman's analysis is a series of questions:

- What are the decision maker's job objectives, and how does he see them?
- What has gone wrong to prevent achieving his objectives?
- What can be added to help him surpass his objectives?
- What resources does the salesman's company possess — in terms of products, service, or know-how—that would enable the decision maker to achieve or surpass his objectives?

The information the salesman requires in order to complete this analysis falls into four distinct categories.

(1) Before he even makes a call, the salesman must have sufficient general information about his product and markets to be able to choose intelligently the customers to approach. This he gains through training, through diligent pre-sale preparation, and through field experience. His final selection of customers to approach is determined by the requirements of his territory sales plan.

(2) Similarly, he must have a wide knowledge of the particular section of industry to which the customer belongs. This again comes from training, pre-sale preparation, and field experience; but familiarity with his existing customers is also important. It is from these customers that he builds up his fund of information on:

- The decision makers' job objectives.
- The systems they used previously.
- The problems they faced under their previous systems.
- The specific reasons they gave for purchasing his product.
- The ways in which his product overcame their problems and the benefits that resulted.
- The other advantages they find in using his product.
- The minor disadvantages they have encountered with his product and the simple ways they have overcome these.

(3) Once he is at the site of the call, he must discover the exact details of the system the customer is using at the moment: *whom* he is ordering from *and why; when* he is ordering *and why; how* the deliveries are made *and why; when* they are made *and why; what* the product is being used for *and why;* the *results* that are being achieved *and why.* In fact, he must gather enough information in all the subdivisions of the present system where a comparison can be made with his own product.

Why is the vital question here, because it provides a qualitative response that indicates the customer's own attitude to his current situation in relation to what is required by his responsibilities.

The salesman uses his questioning technique to identify the gap between what is required and what is achieved. If he can make the customer aware of this gap, the customer will feel dissatisfaction (*cognitive dissonance*) and the motivation to overcome it.

(4) Finally, the salesman must acquire information on the advantages and problems of the present system and on any plans the customer may have for change in the future. The advantages of the present system

can be used to acknowledge the wisdom of the customer's original decision. The problems of the present system, however, are the grist for the salesman's mill, for it is these that will provide the customer with his reasons for change.

The salesman must therefore persevere in his questioning until he is able to establish in detail the disadvantages in the present system.

If he fails to establish disadvantages, logically the customer must be perfectly satisfied with what he has, and the salesman can have no improvement to offer. However, as it is unlikely that this state of perfection exists, the salesman will uncover problem areas. The more he is able to uncover, the more chance he has of ultimately completing the sale; and as the customer talks about his problems, his level of emotional dissatisfaction will grow, since he has now become oriented toward the disadvantages rather than the advantages. The level of emotional dissatisfaction the salesman is able to arouse will determine the speed at which the customer is prepared to reach a decision.

During this period, the salesman, with knowledge of his competitors' products, will be able to suggest problems to the customer, and even ask him why he does not treat certain *inconveniences* as problems. However, it is vital that he not appear to have opinions on the problems. He can ask questions that reveal every aspect of the customer's problems, but he must not give any indication of a personal attitude toward them.

The reason for this is that, by questioning for information, the salesman assumes the role of adviser to the customer. This requires an entirely objective attitude. If the customer feels any subjective interest on the part of the salesman, he will treat him as an antagonist, and this will conflict with the cooperative relationship that is necessary if a fruitful negotiation is to take place.

Seeking information on future plans is always advisable because the salesman can find out, before going any further, whether the customer intends making changes in his system that will exclude products in the field the salesman is offering.

"Actually, we are going out of business next month."

However, if changes are planned that would include his products, the salesman can put forward his proposal as part of the total reorganization. This will help to overcome the customer's natural hesitancy to introduce new suppliers.

As the customer reveals more and more of himself, his plans, and his difficulties, he places himself increasingly in the salesman's hands. The salesman has created a situation in which the sale can progress to the next stage.

The salesman's questions therefore follow the pattern of the categories of information he requires to sell his product.

First, he questions to confirm the general characteristics of the company: size, number of employees, whatever the parameters are that determine whether the company is in the market for his product.

Then he questions to confirm the specific section of the industry the company is in, so that he can begin to decide which product to put forward and which of his existing customers offers the closest comparison in situation to the present customer. This helps him to identify the basic sales arguments he will use later, and to determine the most suitable third-party references.

Then he questions the customer's present methods to confirm the sales arguments he will use, and he modifies them to suit this particular customer.

Finally, his specific questioning on the customer's problem areas determines the precise approach he will take in his proposal and increases the customer's emotional dissatisfaction with his present methods.

The rules for getting information are clear: *Ask questions, take notes* (use a checklist if necessary), *do not make statements, do not introduce the sales proposition.*

The choice of words and phrasing is important. Words like *sign, commitment, order,* and *decision* can evoke fear and reaction if they are used too early in the sale. Used later, they introduce the pressure that is necessary to begin moving the customer toward a decision. Similarly, "would you think" is better than "I think," and "have you considered" is better than "you probably haven't considered." So think it out before you say it. The best single measure of control is to make sure that you ask the questions and he does the talking.

Once the salesman has the information he needs, he is ready to move forward to the next step in the sale, which is to summarize the main points of the conversation so far.

A final point. Quite often, early in the interview, the customer will react to a feeling that he is about to be sold by trying to put you down. He will usually do this by being overly aggressive on some matter of small principle. It is vital not to submit to him. If he can gain control of you at this stage, he will misuse you for the rest of the interview and ultimately fail to make a decision in your favor. The answer is to be quite firm with him and, without becoming involved in an argument, make him understand that you have something to offer and that you are there to speak to him as an equal.

Questioning techniques for control and information

The sales techniques for *getting information* are questioning techniques. Questions provide specific answers, clarify information, and establish control.

By definition, all questions are direct or indirect, open or leading.

	Direct	Indirect
Open		
Leading		

Direct questions are used when you want the customer to know the purpose behind your question:

"Who else is quoting you for this policy?"

Indirect questions are used when you fear that the customer's personal attitude to your question might prejudice his answer:

"What were your main reasons for asking me to quote on this policy exclusively?"

Open questions begin with HOW, WHY, WHEN, WHERE, WHAT, or WHO and elicit a *qualitative* response. Used by the salesman, they tell him what the customer thinks about the subject of the question, and why he thinks it.

Leading questions expecting yes or no or quantitative answers are *manipulative* and are largely used later in the sale to *lead* the customer toward a yes decision.

Whether they are open questions or leading questions, all questions are either direct or indirect. The salesman therefore poses questions beginning HOW, WHY, WHEN, WHERE, WHAT, or WHO in areas where explicit information is important to his subsequent presentation. The customer answers questions on subjects the salesman chooses.

The customer does 90 percent of the talking and enjoys the conversation. The salesman listens and notes. Somewhere in the customer's replies lies the key to the success of the sale.

Leading questions are used at this stage of the sale to establish and maintain control.

If the customer starts talking too much or heading in the wrong direction, the salesman must use a question to interrupt him. This will remove any offense from the interruption. Interrupting with an *open* question will cause the customer to continue talking on a different tack; interrupting with a *leading* question will bring a one-word answer and a pause while he waits for your next question.

The choice between the two types of questions is determined by the requirements of the negotiation at this stage. If you want to make minor alterations in the direction of the customer's conversation, you use an *open* question. If you want to change the subject under discussion completely, you use a *leading* question and follow it with an open question on the new subject. If you think the customer is talking too much or absorbing too much time, you ask him a series of leading questions to increase the tempo of the negotiation.

There is only a limited amount of time available to the salesman for his presentation. He must therefore be rigorous in working to a tight schedule. Not only will this make him more attractively businesslike to the customer, out a good balance and *rhythm* in his presentation will increase his chances of success. A sloppy, time-wasting presentation, on the other hand, will lose the customer's interest well before the *close.*

It is vital that the salesman retain control of the questions at this stage. If the customer returns a question, answer it briefly in general terms and counter it with an open question.

Nine times out of ten the customer will be more interested in answering the new question than in waiting for a full answer to his own question. The tenth time will most likely be a question about product price. It is critical that the salesman successfully delay the full answer to this question until he has had the opportunity to describe the benefits of his product. People buy value, not cost, so they must first know what the product will do.

It is also vital that the salesman understand the complete meaning of the customer's replies to his questions. Any misunderstanding can lead to a breakdown in communication and prejudice the sale. Where he feels that a vital meaning has not been explained in full, the salesman must ask a check question:

"How would this help you?"

Similarly, if he has any doubt as to the real reasoning behind the customer's statement, he must seek clarification with a check question:

"Why is this important to you?"

It is the short road to disaster for the salesman to assume he understands. He must hear the actual words from the customer's mouth.

During this period, the salesman listens carefully to the terms and modes of expression the customer uses to express himself. These will be particular to the customer's trade or industry and are a key to the idiom the salesman must use in his presentation.

If, early in the information-gathering phase of the interview, the customer refuses to answer your question but just sits and looks at you, say nothing yourself until he breaks. Otherwise rephrase your question. If everything else fails, pick a minor dispute with him and, once he starts talking, settle the dispute and continue the sale.

Summarizing information

Once he has asked questions and clarified answers in all areas that he feels are pertinent to his presentation, the salesman should now summarize with the customer the major points that have emerged from their conversation so far.

The reasons for summarizing at this stage are threefold:

- To confirm understanding
- To reidentify the main points
- To make sure nothing has been omitted

This is the first time since he introduced himself that the salesman has really begun to talk. It is the first time that he makes statements, rather than asks questions. The fact that he recounts the main points of the customer's statements, in his own words, confirms that he understands them.

The purpose in reidentifying the main points is to establish the customer's agreement on them. The conversation has been in progress for some minutes now, and the points that were made earlier have tended to become hidden or diminished by those made more recently. By reidentifying them, the salesman reestablishes them equally. By agreeing on them, the customer has committed himself to stand by his statements. This will become important later in the sale if the customer begins to contradict himself.

Finally, he must check to ensure that no major point has been omitted. This is best done with a question. Obviously the information he has received now is going to determine the approach he takes in his presentation. He must try to be sure that he has covered the ground properly.

So the moment he thinks he has the information he needs, the salesman begins his summary:

> "Mr. Chadwick. Just to check that I have fully understood the main points you have made, you said. . . . "

He then summarizes the information in the order in which he requested it:

- General industry information
- Specific company information
- Present system information
- Advantages and disadvantages of the present system

And as he does it he highlights the points he feels will be particularly relevant to his presentation.

Finally, he checks with a direct question to ensure that nothing has been omitted:

> "Is there any other point we have not talked about that you feel is worth mentioning before we go any further?"

Now he is ready to move to the next step in the sale: defining the problem.

The customer's interest is growing. Here at last, he thinks, is someone who understands my problem and knows what he is talking about.

Once you have collected information from the customer and added it to your store of knowledge, you should use it sparingly. Always have something more to say. You can lose a sale by using too little knowledge or too much knowledge, but you will never lose it by using enough knowledge. Treat knowledge as you would a hand of poker. Find out as much as you can about your man without disclosing the cards you hold.

Defining the customer's problem

To define the customer's problem, the salesman now makes a verbal assessment of the advantages and disadvantages of the customer's present system:

> "It would seem from what you have told me about your present system that, *although* you obtain the following advantages: (1) . . . , (2) . . . , (3) . . . , you also suffer from the following disadvantages: (1) . . . , (2) . . . , (3) . . . , (4) . . . . These disadvantages cause you to experience the following problems: (1) . . . , (2) . . . , (3) . . . , which you say are disrupting your operation."

The salesman selects the advantages and disadvantages of the customer's present system carefully from the information the customer has given him. Obviously, he minimizes the advantages against which his products offer a poor comparison; and, similarly, the disadvantages he emphasizes are those against which his product performs strongly.

It is important at this stage that the salesman at least mention the advantages of the present system, because this makes him appear a reliable and unbiased counselor. His strength in taking this course relies on his ability to imply that the disadvantages of the present system outweigh the advantages.

The word *although*, used in the statement of advantages, reduces their value by placing them in comparison with the disadvantages. The disadvantages now become descriptive of what the present system has to offer, and the customer now begins to think and talk about it in these terms.

There is no need for the salesman to exaggerate the disadvantages. This can only reduce his credibility. He needs only to repeat the words and phrases used by the customer himself—"As you said . . ."—and these the customer has to accept.

Now that the statement defining the customer's problem has been made and the customer has accepted it, the salesman is ready to move to the next step in the sale: his statement of intent. The tempo of the sale has increased perceptibly. The customer, from discussing his problem, suddenly finds himself talking business.

The salesman's statement of intent

The statement of intent is the salesman's statement of faith in his product. It carries straight on from the statement defining the customer's problem:

> "There seems to me to be no good reason why you should have to go on putting up with the problems of your present system. I believe I can offer you an alternative which will not only solve your problems but give you a much better final result at only slightly more than your current cost."

Notice that this *salesman's credo* contains nothing that the customer can possibly object to. In fact, he now feels that there just may be an alternative to his current system and he is certainly going to look into it. Already, too, the salesman has become assumptive:

> "I believe I can offer *you* an alternative which *will* not only solve *your* problems but give *you* a much better final result at only slightly more than *your* current cost."

The salesman now continues with a general statement of his sales objective:

> "I mentioned to you that my company has recently brought onto the market a new truck-washing system. I'd like to show you that it *will* provide the solution to all your problems."

If experience warrants it, he might go a step further and define the way he intends to proceed:

> "I think the best way to go about this is for us first to spend a little time talking together about what my product does and the way it does it. Then, if you're satisfied with what I have to say, let's arrange to meet each other at Hankins and Co., just around the corner, so that you can see for yourself that the product does in fact do what I say it will do. Perhaps also, before I leave, I could have a quick look at your site because there is no point in taking your time at a demonstration if there is no place to install the equipment."

All very reasonable and businesslike, isn't it? How can the customer object? But the salesman is assuming that the customer *will* buy his product and has already put him on a decision timetable. Maybe, if he is good, he will close this sale across the table and avoid the demonstration by instead using Eno and Co. as a third-party reference.

Once again, the salesman concludes. This is the last statement he will make until he summarizes the customer's criteria for ordering. Now he is ready to move to the next step in the sale, and the emphasis is again on questions.

6 Establishing the Criteria for Ordering

Establishing the criteria for ordering

It is said that the salesman never sells, the customer only buys. The only way to make the customer buy your product is to make it fit his needs. The only way to find out what he needs is to ask him questions.

Establishing the customer's criteria for ordering is a sales technique by which the salesman, through questions, directs the customer to specify requirements for the new product which, it will turn out, are a close match to the benefits his product is offering.

The questions "What are the factors that are important to you in making your decision?" and "What requirements are you seeking to satisfy with a product like this?" will produce the customer's criteria for ordering. These are basically the needs he is seeking to satisfy in buying a product like yours.

It is essential at this stage in his presentation that the salesman be able to persuade the customer to list all his needs. It is also essential that the salesman understand exactly what the customer says *and* his reasons for saying it.

Initially, the customer will list four or five of the advantages he wants to gain from the new product. He will express himself *in benefit terms:* that is to say, he will list what he wants the product to do for him and what he does not want it to do for him.

He will want at least to retain the better characteristics of his present system and to be rid of its faults.

In his conversation with the salesman so far, the customer has had the chance to clarify in his own mind what is really good and what is really bad about his present system. As he was party to the same conversation, the salesman has already had some opportunity to influence the customer's opinion of what is really good about it and what is really bad. Implicitly, therefore, the customer must already be in part favorably disposed toward the possibilities of the salesman's product although, as yet, he has really heard nothing about it.

The salesman now asks the customer WHY he chose a particular criterion and HOW it is important to him. The customer gives the reasons for his choice and remembers two more criteria he would like to add to his list of requirements.

The salesman sifts these reasons carefully. The statement of the criteria tells him what the customer *says he wants*. The reasons tell him, however, what in fact the customer *needs*.

If the salesman knows he can satisfy a particular need, he congratulates the customer on his wisdom in choosing this need and emphasizes just how important it is. Similarly, if he can satisfy the need, but in a slightly different way from the one the customer has in mind, he shows that this is really the better way to look at it *in terms of the overall product concept!*

If, on the other hand, the salesman knows he cannot satisfy the particular need with his product, he shows that this need is not of great importance and is anyhow *outweighed* by the customer's more serious requirements.

In this way, the salesman starts constructing with the customer a list of criteria to be satisfied, and placing them in an order of importance. The order of importance he is seeking to establish is defined by the particular blend of benefits his product offers. However, at this stage, negotiation is still centered on the customer's requirements: what is and is not an advantage, and what is and is not a disadvantage. He still does not mention the characteristics of his own product.

As the conversation continues and the customer begins to run out of ideas, the salesman starts to introduce the other needs the customer should be seeking to satisfy.

He is, it should be remembered, the expert in the specific subject under negotiation. His product will bring about innovation in the customer's methods, and his role is to ensure that the customer is fully aware of all its implications.

The new needs he now adds to the customer's list of criteria are the ones his product is particularly good at satisfying. The needs his product satisfies exclusively are the ones whose satisfaction makes a new decision not only worthwhile but imperative. Other needs that competition happens to satisfy are barely mentioned except to show that, in the customer's particular case, they are simply unimportant and not worth satisfying.

Competition, if it arrives in time, now has the more difficult problem of changing the customer's opinion rather than making it. Conversation continues to be confined to needs. Products are still not mentioned and the existence of competition is not suggested, let alone named.

Questions introduce the new needs:

> "What about vehicle cleanliness? Do you think it's important for the new equipment to be fast enough to give you cleanliness any time the vehicle returns from its journey?"

Questions develop meaning:

> "What exactly do you mean by cleanliness? Do you want commercial cleanliness for good advertising, or do you really want the vehicles to be spotless?"

And questions develop implication:

> "In what ways is vehicle cleanliness particularly important to you?"

The questions are a combination of *open* and *leading* questions as the salesman forces the customer to commit himself to decisions in all the subareas that are covered by the product. Handled correctly, all these decisions will be favorable to the salesman.

In this way the salesman establishes the customer's criteria for ordering (*the customer's compromise*), and as he listens to the customer's replies he notes the words and terms he uses to express himself. These are the words and terms the salesman is going to use in his presentation.

The compromise he persuades the customer to accept must be a close match to his product. If you find that, despite your efforts, you cannot make this match, or that the customer just will not talk business with you, the negotiation cannot proceed. There will be no firm basis for it. It is better to pack your bags and leave politely—even if he asks you to tell him about your product anyway. Your time is better spent with a customer who will talk business with you.

The salesman now summarizes the criteria for ordering, giving reasons why each of them is important:

> "May I now confirm with you that these are the criteria you are seeking to satisfy in your decision? First you said that... was of the utmost importance to you because.... Second, ..."

Then he asks a final open question to make sure no criteria are omitted:

> "What are the other factors we have omitted?"

It is vital that all the customer's criteria be established now. If another requirement appears later in the sale, particularly one the salesman cannot satisfy, it is likely to bring the sales presentation crashing to the ground.

Once the customer says yes, these are all the factors, and no, none have been omitted, the salesman is in a position to proceed with his presentation.

In a normal two-way sales conversation, there is no harm in your occasionally being wrong. In fact, it may even be a good idea now and then to let the customer show that he is right. So if there is a point you are not sure of, present it as a question and get his opinion. Alternatively, tell him that he has been in the industry much longer than you and ask him for his advice. It is much better than clinging to assertions you can barely support.

At any meeting during a sale, it is possible to find yourself talking to a customer who is dull, obstinate, and indecisive. There is a way of handling him which, with cool courage and good balance, can be very successful. It is simply to pick an argument with him.

It usually comes when you are defining the customer's problem and the factors that are important in his decision. The customer will for some personal reason not agree to a point that is logical and reasonable. You question him to find the reason, without success. Unless you reach agreement on the point, you cannot proceed with the sale and reasonably expect a decision.

When you know the arguments are on your side, take issue on the point. Insist that he take your view. Make him involve himself. Twist him and drag him until you are sure he has a good grip on the bone; then settle with him. Offer him agreement or an alternative that has not so far been considered.

The effect of a sudden and reasonable settlement is to make him your friend for the rest of the sale. He will now try to understand and agree to everything else you have to say. You have raised the emotional content of the dialog and prepared him to place his order.

The customer's compromise

Every decision we ever make involves some level of compromise. We seldom find a product or service that provides us with everything we want; and, even when we do, it usually costs a little more than we really intended to pay.

Besides, with the inexorable march of progress and the multiplication of services available to us, whatever we do decide to acquire is seldom the up-to-date latest for long. It seems that no sooner do we make one decision than something faster, more efficient, cheaper, and more beautiful comes along.

Unfortunately, that is just a fact of life. The answer cannot be to avoid all decisions—though it is true that products and services in their most perfect form will be found in paradise. We have to satisfy our requirements while we live, and accept that one decision will ultimately replace a previous one, and so on.

The way we see and specify our needs is strictly personal, although our differing needs are often satisfied by the same product. For example, one man may buy a car to satisfy a need to ride in comfort as he goes about his business, while another may buy the same car because he thinks it will improve his position on the social scale.

And then, having made our decision and our purchase, our priorities change. Now we seek to provide a solution to the next most pressing problem in our life.

The product we bought, however, itself changes our view of what our requirements really are. You only have to buy one car to realize just how nice other cars are, and so it becomes a matter of time before the initial requirements come up for review.

None of us is different. We are all customers; and the customers we are seeking to persuade are people too.

The implications for the salesman are clear:

- He must be able to understand the importance the customer attaches to the satisfaction of each of his needs, in order to be able to establish *communication* with him.
- He must be able to reconstruct the order and importance of each of these needs in such a way that he will be able to show the customer that he will achieve greater satisfaction through the acquisition of the product he is offering.
- He must be able to adjust the customer's definition of his needs so that he will be able to show how the customer's very important, basic needs will be met by the benefits of his product, while at the same time he shows how the needs he cannot meet are really unimportant.
- He must be able to create strong new needs for the special benefits his product offers as an innovation to the current system.
- He must be able to show that the new satisfactions his product offers are of such importance to the customer that he cannot afford to delay his decision.
- He must be able to show the customer that the new product will add significant value to his system, so that when he comes to the discussion of price later in the sale he will have no trouble in showing that the expenditure is worthwhile.

Matching the customer's decision criteria to the product

Let us see how the salesman matches the customer's decision criteria to the features his product is offering. The chart (pages 100–101) shows the relation of the salesman's product to the customer's present system. The salesman opens the dialog:

S. If you were to acquire a new truck-washing facility, what requirements would you be seeking to satisfy?
C. I'd want a machine at least as fast as the present system, but one which would wash the front and back as well. We've also had a lot of trouble holding the men who work the equipment, particularly during the winter, when the trucks are dirtiest.

So the next time we would want the machine to be automatic. Of course, the cost would have to be within reason.

S. Why is speed so important to you?

C. Our fleet operates on retail delivery, and these deliveries must be completed by 10:00 every morning. The result is that between 9:45 and 11:00 every morning the whole fleet returns to the depot, and we like to wash them before we park them for the day. If we can't wash each truck quickly enough, either we have to bring them back to be washed during the day, which is expensive, or we have a line of trucks blocking the street, waiting for their turn in the wash.

S. I notice that you have trucks in a number of different sizes. Your present system doesn't wash the front or back either, does it?

C. No, that's another problem. The small sales trucks really have to be washed by hand, and we can't do that as often as we'd like. You're quite right when you say the present system does not wash the front or back. If we try to do this by hand, we again end up delaying the return of the vehicles. So we split them into three groups; which means we wash the front and back of each truck every third day.

S. Is this enough?

C. Of course it isn't. The front's all right but it's the back that picks up all the mud and grime. That should really be washed daily. In fact, sometimes I'm quite ashamed at the state of our fleet.

S. I can understand your feelings, particularly since your trucks carry food. How long does it take to wash a truck all over by your present methods?

C. About six minutes.

S. If the truck could be washed all over in three minutes when it came in, would it cause the delay you mentioned?

C. No. Three minutes would be fine. (*Salesman overcomes basic washtime disadvantage*)

S. You mentioned your labor problems. How many men do you have to employ and what do they cost you?

C. Well, if we're going to do the job properly, we need two men who more or less work full time with the trucks. They must cost together $240 per week at least.

Product feature	What the product does
Fast	Washes in less than 3 minutes
Washes any shape or size of vehicle	Washing frame descends around vehicle
Washes front, back, roof, and sides	Washing frame descends around vehicle
Washes every nook and cranny (exclusive advantage)	Liquid action wash
Automatic	Button controlled by one man
High shine and corrosion-resistant finish	Chemical additives
No damage to vehicle—wash action actually benefits it (exclusive advantage)	Solely liquid action—no brushes
No corrosion to equipment	Aluminum
Inexpensive maintenance	Made up of simple inexpensive parts
Does not freeze in winter	Plastic pipes, and protected by chemicals
Inexpensive to operate	Weekly lease terms and chemical charges

Benefits to the customer	Salesman's knowledge of customer's present system
Washes vehicles every time they return to depot No backup problems resulting from uneven vehicle return Cleaner vehicles through more frequent washing Frequent washing reduces salt corrosion	Faster drive-through wash
Washes all types of vehicles equally well in same equipment	Washes well only slab-sided vehicles within certain size range
Washes roof, front, and back at same time as sides No additional time or labor	Man has to wash front and back, slowing down speed through the system Roof never washed
Liquid action washes every bolt and rivet hole, wheel hubs, oily door hinges, etc. Vehicle looks really clean, not just hastily washed	Gives overall wash but leaves rivet holes, wheel hubs, oily door hinges, etc., obviously uncleaned
Minimum of costly labor Anyone can operate it without hardship Washes all year round	Labor-intensive if you want front and back washed too Special team required Men won't work in wintry conditions
Windows dry free from watermarks: no additional polishing Paintwork dries with high shine while corrosion inhibitor protects metal	Windows must be washed separately Paintwork dulled and damaged by brush action
Gentler action of wash lengthens time span between paint resprays and therefore saves money Vehicle looks better longer	Machine removes wipers, wing mirrors, and chrome strips, which can further damage bodywork
Cheaper maintenance—less replacement	Steel parts corrode badly
Inexpensive and simple to maintain	Breakdown leads to heavy cost and long shutdown periods
All-year-round operation	Machine becomes inoperable because of freezing at low temperatures
Can be shown to have lower wash cost per vehicle Exact weekly wash costs known	Labor and maintenance costs increasingly prohibitive Actual vehicle wash costs unknown

S. That's quite a lot of money to pay when you don't get the cleanliness you want. Presumably, if the machine was simple enough and automatic, you could arrange for the first driver home to operate it?

C. Yes. Actually, I hadn't thought of it like that but I suppose you're right.

S. That would mean a saving of $240 a week.

C. Yes, that's right.

S. How do you wash *that* truck?

C. Don't mention it to me. It's been nothing but a problem since we bought it. At the moment we have to detail one man to wash it once a week. It's used to carry eggs for the cakes. It takes the man about a day just to get the spilled albumen off. If you can wash that truck, believe me, you have yourself a sale. (*Throws hands into air*)

S. What about paint damage?

C. Well, we have no problems with this. We keep a truck four years and respray it three times in this period. I think you'd agree that, when they're clean, the trucks really look very smart.

S. Yes, they certainly do. However, what would it be worth if we could in fact save you one of those paint resprays?

C. You can work it out for yourself. Under the contract we have, each truck costs an average of $300 to respray, and we have forty-five trucks.

S. Are you considering changing that color scheme, although I must say it's very smart?

C. Yes, that's going to be another problem. The advertising idea now is to move to white vehicles by the end of the year, which is going to make cleaning a real problem. I must say I like the dark green; but what else can I say, I chose it.

S. You mentioned labor problems and winter washing. What about the equipment freezing?

C. Yes, that's a problem too. In fact, that's where the labor problem starts. When it gets really cold, the machine freezes up and the trucks have to be washed with a hose. Soon everything gets covered with water, which then turns to ice. The men start slithering around all over the place; and really, quite rightly, they decide they can get a better job elsewhere.

S. And the trucks go uncleaned until new men are employed?

C. And the trucks go uncleaned.

S. You said the cost of the new system would have to be within reason. Remembering that it cost $3.00 to have your car washed, do you think $1.80 a truck per wash would be too much? (*If the customer objects, the salesman can bring in the saving in labor and truck-painting costs. The customer is spending over $240 a week on labor alone and he does not have clean trucks.*)

C. No. That's really very good. I certainly couldn't wash one of our trucks myself for $1.80.

S. Good. Is there anything we've left out?

C. No.

S. If I may summarize our conversation so far, *when* you buy a new machine, it will have to meet several requirements:

— It must provide a high standard of cleanliness, even in winter, so you have no cause to be ashamed of the trucks that carry your company name.

— It must wash all the different shapes and sizes of trucks you have, all over, at one time, so you have all your trucks clean at any one time, rather than most of them half clean.

— It must wash the trucks quickly enough when they return from delivery so you get no blocking in the street. Although you would like equipment as fast as your present system, the requirement is for a wash to be completed in about three minutes.

— It must wash the trucks with a simple automatic system that a driver can use, so you can break your dependence on the labor that is giving you so much trouble besides costing you $240 a week.

— It must save one respray if possible, though you do not see this as a particular problem.

— It must operate without freezing up or catching the flu in winter.

— And, finally, you would like to achieve this at a total unit wash cost of around $1.80. Would you agree with this?

C. There's one other point. Whenever the present system breaks down, we seem to be involved in heavy replacement costs.

I must say that has become a significant item of expenditure on our current wash bill. I would certainly like to avoid that in the future.

S. So you would like to add the requirement for simple, inexpensive maintenance to the list?

C. That's right. Otherwise, I think you have summarized exactly what we are looking for.

S. (*Now looking for a date deadline*) Presumably, you want the new machine installed by the time the redecorating work is done on the fleet?

C. Certainly. In fact, the sooner the better.

S. Good. If I could provide you with a machine that would meet your requirements, would you be prepared to place your order with me? (*Trial close*)

C. Of course. What else could I say?

Assumptive selling

Assumption is basic to the art of persuasion. The persuader must always assume in his dialog that the respondent will ultimately take the course he is proposing and that negotiation is really a matter of ironing out the details.

The salesman first assumes, in his presentation, that the customer will make a new decision to buy. This helps the customer *see* change as inevitable and so overcome his natural reluctance to alter his existing methods.

The salesman then assumes, in Stages 2 and 3 of the sale, that the customer will make the particular decision to buy and use the product the salesman is selling. This helps the customer *see* the benefits that will accrue from the new product, and so simplifies the decision itself.

Assumptive selling also helps the customer actually to visualize the benefits of your product in operation. Once he has added these images to his memory bank, the decision itself will tend to become a mere formality. He will already have come to expect the benefits of the new product, and will become increasingly dissatisfied with his old methods.

In Stage 1 of the sale, during the questioning involved in *getting information* and *establishing the criteria for ordering*, the technique for selling assumptively is to preface as many questions as you can with the word *when* rather than *if*.

> *"When* you buy the new product, what are the advantages you want to gain from it?"

In Stages 2 and 3 of the sale, as the salesman moves from questions to statements in selling benefits and overcoming objections, the assumptive technique requires that he continue to use the word *when* to preface his statement, and also that he cover the nouns with the possessive adjectives *my* and *your*.

> *"When* you install *my* product, you will find *your* staff will have none of these burdensome problems. Instead, they will enjoy. . . ."

Obviously, the better the salesman can now paint the word picture of the customer's staff flushed with a new enjoyment in using his products, the more likely he is to succeed in implanting that picture, and therefore the purchase required to make that picture a reality, firmly in the customer's head.

Whether he chooses to talk to the customer about his staff, his personal or company image, or his freedom from worry will depend largely on his assessment of the customer's psychological makeup (see the section "The Human Motivational Factors" in Chapter 3).

Always sell assumptively.

Summarizing the criteria for ordering

The summary of the criteria for ordering draws a line under this step in the sale. It confirms that the questioning in this area is complete:

> "May I now confirm with you that these are the criteria you are seeking to satisfy in your decision? First, you said that . . . was of the utmost importance to you because. . . . Second, ..."

The customer will obviously object if he feels that he has been misinterpreted in any way, and the meaning will be clarified.

The salesman now asks:

"Are there any other factors we have omitted?"

The customer now brings forward any other criteria that he wants considered. The salesman questions him for meaning, weighs and ranks these criteria in relation to the criteria that have already been discussed, and adds them to his list.

It is of course vital that he be successful in establishing every important criterion now. The agreement that will be reached in this summary will form the basis of Stage 2 of the sale.

The line that is drawn by agreement on the decision criteria must be argument-proof. As the sale proceeds, and the customer comes under increasing pressure, the salesman must always be in a position to say:

"I understand the point you are making, but we agreed earlier that. . . ."

However, the customer can say at any time:

"Ah, but we didn't talk about this . . ."

or

"Ah, but that is not what I meant."

In that case, the salesman either has not agreed upon the full list of criteria or has not established the exact meaning of all his terms. The line drawn under this step in the sale is then broken and the basis on which Stage 2 of the sale depends is lost.

The customer comes under increasing pressure as he is moved toward the decision. He will almost inevitably try to avoid a decision today on the pretext that it is better made tomorrow (*by which time he will have found a reason to avoid it altogether*).

In his attempt to escape a conclusion, the customer will inevitably return to test the basis on which the salesman's presentation is made. If he manages to find a loophole, nine times out of ten he will use it to make his escape. The salesman can only attempt to reestablish the original agreements between them. Otherwise, he will risk having the sale degenerate into an argument. Whatever he does, through either relief at escaping or exhaustion from time already spent, the customer is unlikely to let the negotiation begin again.

The trial close to establish commitment

Once the summary of the criteria for ordering has been agreed upon between customer and salesman, the salesman makes his first trial close:

> S. *If I* could provide a system that would meet all these require-
> ments that you have given me, *would you* be prepared to
> place your order with me?
> C. If the price is right, yes.

What else can the customer say? After all, the criteria are the ones he has listed, and even the words the salesman has used to summarize them were his own. If the customer says "No," the salesman can ask "Why not?"

The salesman here has a safety mechanism through which he can confirm whether or not all the decision criteria have been fully disclosed.

The customer is likely now to disclose the remaining hidden criteria. On the other hand, he may become hesitant in order to avoid making any commitment to a decision. In this case, the salesman must pursue the question:

> "Why not? Surely these are the criteria that you yourself have
> given me as being important to your decision?"

The customer is hesitating because there is something he does not want to tell the salesman. Perhaps he is not the decision maker. Perhaps the company is going out of business. Perhaps the whole operation is changing and there will not be a demand for the new product. Whatever it is, the salesman must find it out now. There is absolutely no point in his proceeding with his presentation until the situation has been clarified. If the reasons for the customer's hesitancy are any of those mentioned, the presentation will have to be discontinued diplomatically and the negotiation reestablished with the decision maker at a better place at a better time.

If the customer says:

> "Well, I don't really want to become involved in a decision now
> but I would certainly be interested in hearing about what you
> have to offer,"

the salesman must continue to press for commitment:

> "You have dirty trucks now and you need a good truck-washing
> facility now. You are already spending a lot of money and
> you have told me you are not getting the cleanliness you want
> for your expenditure. If I can solve your truck-cleaning prob-
> lem, surely now is a good time to reach a decision on it?"

If he still fails to achieve commitment, he can only conclude. There
is no point in going on with the negotiation if he cannot take the decision now. He will only prejudice the sale in the future. His time
anyway is better spent with a customer who is in a position to buy.

> S. Well, there's no point in discussing the details of the product
> now if you want to make a decision in the future. By that
> time your requirements, and the price, will probably have
> changed. When will you want to make your decision?
>
> C. We'll definitely want to have a machine installed by next
> July, when all the trucks will have the new color scheme.
>
> S. Well, if I may, I'll telephone you next March, and we can begin
> our discussions again.

Or

> Well, frankly, this would seem to be the right time to make
> your decision. If you're able to place your order now, we'll
> hold today's prices; and we'll also be able to arrange de-
> livery and installation the exact day you want the machine.
> Obviously, if between now and next March you change your
> mind, we are not going to install the equipment against
> your wishes—and we'll cancel the order. I am quite happy
> to give you a letter to this effect.

If the salesman succeeds in this tactic, he is likely to take the order with little trouble. In effect, he has removed any objection to the decision. The customer is safe to place his order, in fact whether he wants the equipment or not. However, having made a decision, he is unlikely to change his mind and the equipment will then see installation.

The purpose of the trial close at this stage is therefore to bring commitment into the negotiation. The customer knows the salesman will ultimately ask for the order, and perhaps more important, the salesman knows the customer expects him to ask for the order.

The technique by which this commitment is obtained, by persuading the customer first to list his criteria and then to stand by his list, ensures that the customer will have few objections to accepting the commitment.

The form of the trial close is the question in the conditional:

"*If I* do this, *would you* do that?"

The trial close is used from now on throughout the sale to establish agreement and maintain commitment.

7 Prehandling Objections

The role of objections in the sale

Objections come at any time in the sale when the customer interrupts the presentation to ask a question. Something is troubling him. Either he wants more information, or he is not fully satisfied with the answers the salesman is giving him, or he is worried about continuing the conversation lest it lead to a decision.

It is obviously vital that the salesman be able to assess the nature of these questions (as well as the possible consequences of his answers). He must be able to evaluate whether the question is sincere or merely disruptive, whether it should be answered now or later. Once the customer manages to lead him down a blind alley, the salesman will from that moment lose control, and he may never be able to regain it.

Equally, the salesman, as far as possible, will want to influence the questions that are asked and when they are asked. Unplanned interruptions from the customer can disturb the sequence of his presentation and reduce its effectiveness.

However, objections perform a very valuable function in the sale. For example, they show the salesman:

- The way the customer is reacting to the form of his presentation.
- The way the customer is reacting to the information contained in his presentation.
- The areas that need special clarification.
- The obstacles that remain to be overcome before the customer feels able to commit himself to a final decision.

111

— The way the customer is reacting to the increasing pressure the salesman is putting on him to make a decision.

Objections therefore fall into four categories:

— Problems of attitude.
— Requests for further information.
— Sincere obstacles to which the customer feels he must find satisfactory answers before he can make a decision.
— Insincere obstacles, matters usually of minor importance, that the customer will exaggerate if he is allowed to bring them up later in the sale in order to escape from a decision.

Problems of customer attitude must be monitored throughout the sales presentation. Obviously, the salesman is taking unnecessary risks if he appears in front of the customer in clothes that are remarkable, if he adopts poses that could be offensive, or if he expresses opinions (even about the local football team) that could be disputable. His appearance and posture should take the risk only of pleasing. He should rely on his friendliness, his business acumen, and his concern with the customer's problems to build the customer's good opinion of him. The words he uses should be the words the customer has used to express himself in the earlier stages of *getting information* and *establishing the criteria for ordering.*

Otherwise, the salesman must watch the customer's face closely for any signs of distress. If the customer appears uninterested, the salesman must ask:

"How important would this be to you?"

If the customer appears distracted, the salesman must ask:

"Is there something I should have mentioned that I have left out?"

And if the customer appears disquieted, the salesman must ask:

"Have I covered that point fully enough for you?"

The trick is to use questions to bring the customer back into the conversation, at the same time retaining control by retaining the choice of questions.

Requests for information are natural throughout the sale as the customer seeks further clarification. Obviously the salesman can in part influence the questions that are asked by his decision whether to provide information in a particular area. The skillful salesman may deliberately leave information gaps in areas where his product offers special benefits in the hope that the customer will ask a question in that area and discover that benefit for himself. On the other hand, he will meticulously conceal areas where a difficult, unwanted question might pin him against the wall.

Experience will soon teach the salesman the types of question he can expect. Some will be simple questions of detail which he will answer right away. Others will cause warning lights to flash, and to make sure that he fully understands the implications of a question before he attempts to answer it, the salesman will ask:

> "Why do you ask that?"

Some questions he will preempt by providing information. Some he will preempt by indicating when he will provide information:

> "The question of price I'll come to later when I have described the process to you and had the chance to determine fully the specifications you will require."

Finally, for some questions that come up out of place, he will seek postponement until he can provide the answer without breaking the sequence of his presentation:

> "I was just coming to that point."

Or

> "I'd like to come back to price after I've described the process to you and had the chance to find out the specifications you require. Frankly, I don't think price is going to be a problem."

The sincere obstacles to which the customer feels he must find a satisfactory answer before he can make a final decision come later in the sale. Generally, they come when the salesman says:

"Shall we now go ahead and place your order?"

and the customer replies:

"I'd like to go ahead except for. . . . "

These are the final objections in the sale. They are sincere; if the salesman succeeds in overcoming them, he will take the order. (The final objections are discussed fully in Chapter 11.)

The insincere obstacles are objections that the customer tries to create and magnify in order to disrupt the salesman and escape the decision. From experience, the salesman knows what they are. If he can bring them into the negotiation while he is establishing the criteria for ordering, he can nullify them by winning the customer's agreement, at that time, that they will not constitute an obstacle later in the sale. If he omits this precaution, there is every likelihood that the objection will spring back into the negotiation at the *close* stage. Then the customer will argue that he must go away and think about it; and there will be nothing the salesman can do to persuade him otherwise.

It is therefore the insincere objections, matters of minor importance that carry the risk of being inflated out of proportion later in the sale, that must be *prehandled* before the salesman can safely move to Stage 2 of his presentation.

The objections to prehandle

In every sale there are objections that are better prehandled. In every sales presentation, therefore, the salesman should devote a certain amount of time to *prehandling objections*. This time should be allocated during the period when he is establishing the criteria for ordering.

It is only when the salesman has prehandled objections (and handled competition) that he can afford to move to Stage 2 of the sale.

Prehandling objections is achieved by introducing the objection before the customer thinks of it, providing the answer, and then getting the customer's agreement that the answer is satisfactory.

Once the customer agrees on the answer to an objection, it is difficult for him to reintroduce the objection later in the sale. If he does, the salesman need only remind him of his previous agreement:

"But you said earlier that you accepted . . . . "

Obviously, when he is prehandling objections, the salesman must make sure that he fully understands the customer's potential objection and that he does provide the suitable answer. The exact implication of the potential objection, and therefore the answer, will vary according to the type of customer and his specific requirements; and only questions will check these.

If the customer subsequently breaks agreements made at this stage in the sale, he breaks a faith that is implicit in any negotiation. As there is then no firm basis on which the negotiation can continue, the salesman can only conclude and leave.

The objections that should be prehandled fall into the following categories:

- Objections based on hesitancy or reluctance to make a decision now.
- Objections based on the customer's opinion that his is a special case.
- Objections based on the availability of a competitive alternative.
- Objections based on hearsay.
- Objections based on price.
- Objections based on the new set of circumstances the customer will face if he buys the new product.

The moment at which the salesman chooses to prehandle an objection will depend on the gravity of the potential objection and his ability to provide a satisfactory solution. If the potential objection is grave but the salesman can provide the full solution, he will prehandle the objection while he establishes the customer's criteria for ordering, and he will probably include the solution in his summary of this stage of the sale. On the other hand, if the potential objection is minor in nature, or if the salesman's solution is not as conclusive as he would like it to be, he will prehandle the objection after he has summarized the criteria for ordering. At this point, the customer will be eager to go on to the benefit selling stage, and the salesman has the opportunity to gloss over the objection and its solution.

Prehandling objections

Objections based on hesitancy or reluctance to make a decision now

These objections are caused by:

- Reluctance to make a decision that will exclude the possibility of an alternative and, perhaps, a better decision later.
- Fear of changing from a known method to a new method that is not fully understaood.
- Natural disinclination to spend money.
- Fear of making the wrong decision.

The technique the salesman uses is to recognize the objection by asking a right question now that will preempt a wrong statement from the customer later in the sale. This question also retains control in the hands of the salesman, whereas a wrong statement at the wrong time could disrupt his presentation and throw him off balance.

The salesman's right question:

"*If* the product *I* am offering is the one you are looking for, *are you* prepared to make your decision immediately?"

preempts the customer's wrong statement:

"I'd like to think it over."

The salesman's question is really a trial close to obtain commitment.

The salesman's right question:

"When will you want it by?"

preempts the customer's wrong statement:

"I won't need it for a few months yet."

Here, what the customer is really saying is that he would prefer to think about it again later. Of course, by that time, another salesman from a different company will already have taken his order.

Alternatively, to prehandle the same objection, the salesman may be more assumptive and, in effect, introduce a decision criterion related to the date of purchase:

> "You will probably want it installed in time for next winter?"

Or

> "Presumably, you will want to make your decision in time for your October purchasing budget?"

If the salesman can obtain a commitment to a date of installation or delivery, he is then in a position to show the customer how he can and why he should place his order now. If, on the other hand, it is obvious that no decision will be taken until a later date, the salesman can only suggest an approximate date for the new appointment and curtail his presentation.

The salesman's right question:

> "What do you have in mind?"

preempts the customer's wrong statement:

> "It's not quite what I had in mind."

Really, in this instance, the salesman is doing no more than asking the customer to identify his criteria for ordering.

The salesman's right question:

> "Are you able to make this decision alone, or must you put it before your partners?"

preempts the customer's wrong statement:

> "I must put the decision before my partners."

It is always worthwhile for the salesman to ask a similar question to confirm that he is in fact negotiating with the decision maker. If the decision really must go before partners or a Board, the salesman can suggest a joint meeting; or he can adjust his presentation to take the order on a provisional basis, subject to Board approval.

The questions the salesman asks now in order to prehandle objections based on hesitancy are vital if he is to receive the customer's decision for his product across the table.

Objections based on the customer's opinion that his is a special case

Every salesman has met customers who think that their problems are special and defy the normal solutions. (The objection, "It doesn't apply in my case," will be the most common objection to this book.) Of course, this is just nonsense. But if the salesman waits for the customer to say, later in the sale,

> "My particular case is different from most, and you probably do not fully understand it,"

he finds himself in the impossible situation of having to show the customer why his case is no different from the rest and why he really does understand it. Unfortunately, at the same time, he shows the customer that he is wrong. The tendency then is for the negotiation to break away from the vital matters of common concern and to dissolve into unnecessary dispute.

The salesman can preempt the customer's wrong statement by saying at this state in the sale:

> "Of course, no two companies, even in the same industry, are alike. But when it comes to vehicle washing, they all have the one problem in common: how to wash their vehicles simply, quickly, and cheaply so that they know they have, and can afford to have, clean vehicles on the streets. This surely must be your problem too?"

It is essential that the salesman keep away from intercompany and interindustry differences and concentrate his comments on the things products in his market can or cannot do. In this area, he is the undisputed expert.

Objections based on the availability of a competitive alternative

The customer has four alternative courses of action available to him:

- To do nothing
- To spend his money on something entirely different
- To buy a directly competitive product
- To buy your product

Obviously, your objective is that he elect to buy your product. While you are making your presentation, you have a unique opportunity to persuade him to take this one course. The moment you leave without his order, the other three courses of action become realistic alternatives to him.

You should therefore try to *close* a customer's order at every interview. If you leave without it, you have set him up for a competitor. You have created needs without satisfying them. Also, the longer the customer takes to make a decision, the more he becomes used to doing without your product and the less likely he is ultimately to make a decision in your favor. Certainly, unless you *close* at every interview, you can never really know that you have taken the shortest route, which is the best route, to the order.

The salesman must overcome the customer's natural resistance to making a decision and persuade him of the importance of an immediate decision. There are several ways he can achieve this:

- He can emphasize the importance of the decision and the value that it will bring immediately, both to the customer himself and to his company.
- He can show that, in terms of the value of the customer's time and the relative unimportance of the matter under discussion, the decision is not worth not making now.
- He can stress to the customer that, although he gets by with his present system, there is now no need for him to continue to put up with all its problems: there are just better ways available to achieve the same result.

He bolsters this argument with *word pictures* of things as they might be and with references to other companies that have found life better with the new system.

The technique the salesman uses to achieve this purpose is to ask direct questions which effectively transfer to the customer the opinion of value or importance for each of his decision criteria that the salesman wants him to have. The customer readily accepts the salesman's opinion at this stage because the salesman appears to be confirming an excellent choice of decision criteria rather than coercing the customer to accept the same opinion.

Thus, as he establishes each of the customer's criteria for ordering, the salesman seeks agreement on value or importance with questions such as these:

"Well, if you could only achieve this result, it would be worthwhile installing the new product right away, wouldn't it?"

"Considering the industry you are in, it is of daily importance that you do have clean vehicles on the road, isn't it?"

"In terms of your total involvement in this area and the importance of the decisions you must be making, the subject I am discussing with you is hardly worth a second meeting, is it?"

"From what you have told me, as long as the expenditure is within reason, it is just not worthwhile to go on putting up with all these problems, is it? There must be better ways to do things?"

These assumptive questions are used by the salesman to sell against the possibility that the customer will choose to do nothing, or to spend his money on something entirely different. The best way to sell against the alternative of a competitive product, however, is not to mention it (this is discussed in Chapter 8).

Objections based on hearsay

Once a product has been established in a market, opinions pass around about it—what it should do that it does not do, what it can and cannot do, and so on. This is inevitable since consumers throughout the country in similar activities meet in associations and institutes and read the same journals.

The salesman who recognizes the role of hearsay tries to influence it to act in his favor. He works as best he can to ensure that his product message is clearly understood by his customers and, perhaps, is passed on to their friends and associates in other companies. In this way, he hopes to generate inquiries.

Unfortunately, as most gossip tends to concentrate on disasters, there is a very good chance that the customer has heard something to the detriment of your product. Often it is no more than rumor, and blatantly untrue. If the salesman waits for the customer to bring it up, it can cause disruption to the sales presentation. On the other hand, if the salesman himself brings it up and the rumor is new to the customer, it can cause fresh and unwarranted fears.

The safest course for the salesman to take is to create a situation in which the customer is able to repeat any rumor he has heard. He can do this by asking the customer if he has heard of the product before or if he knows any company that is using it.

If the customer has heard neither of the product nor of companies that are using it, the salesman has a good chance to introduce as references for his product the names of happy users who are known to the customer.

If, on the other hand, the customer knows a company that is using the product, the salesman must decide whether this company is a good reference or not. If it is a good reference, he can ask the customer whether he knows how the company is doing with it. Alternatively, he can frankly detail the advantages this company has found with his product, and even suggest that the new customer telephone to confirm what he says. Usually, the suggestion alone is sufficient.

If the company is a doubtful reference, the salesman can preempt the customer's statement of what he has heard by mentioning himself some of the simpler problems this company has had and, frankly, the mistakes it has made to cause them. He would at the same time, however, emphasize the real advantages the company has experienced with the product. Then, even if the customer decides to telephone this company, which is unlikely, the chances are that it will support its original decision. Anyway, the customer's understanding of any comments the company makes will be colored by what the salesman has had to say in his explanation.

What the customer says and what the customer knows may be two different things. Good questioning by the salesman will cause the customer to make explicit what he knows.

If the customer tells of a rumor, or the salesman suspects he has heard it, the salesman must confront it and discount it. One way he can do this is by treating it as a rumor:

C. Someone was saying the other day that the washing frame of your machine was always falling and catching the vehicle inside it.

S. I know this has been said, although I have never seen it happen. Frankly, if this really was a problem of substance, we could never have sold so many machines. In fact, we probably would not have been allowed by law to produce them.

An alternative way to prehandle this type of objection is to mention it as a problem your other well-known and satisfied customers do not have:

"This company now has five units installed, and another five on order. If the product represented a hazard to their employees in any way, they really would not allow it into their factories."

Objections based on hearsay are inevitable when any product has an established market. Obviously, competition too is going to make the most out of them. However, from the salesman's point of view, it is easier to sell into an established market than to establish a market. Selling into a market when you have no third-party references is much more difficult than prehandling occasional objections based on hearsay.

Objections based on price

Price is the final objection in any sale. At the end of the presentation, the customer will want to weigh the benefits he understands he will obtain from the product against the cost he understands he will have to pay. In this way, he will make his estimate of the value of the salesman's proposition.

The customer will pay the price if, in his value judgment, the price is right. Obviously, he will have to know the benefits before he can understand their value. So benefit selling must always come before price discussion in the sales presentation. Inevitably, he will ask questions to obtain an idea of price range in the meantime, but the salesman must succeed in putting him off:

"May I come back to price in a minute?"

Or

> "Less than it costs you to run your refrigerator."

Or

> "Less than 50¢ a day, but let me be more specific when I know the precise specifications you will want."

If the salesman weakens and gives the price away before he has sold the benefits of his product, the customer will shut his mind to the rest of the presentation, whether the price is favorable or not. Result: no sale. Nobody ever buys a cost, even a lower one!

However, a great part of the price battle is fought at this stage of the sale. While the salesman is establishing the customer's criteria for ordering, he can begin to influence the customer's judgment of *value*. In effect he is prehandling a price objection which he knows he will have to face later in his presentation. The higher he can build the customer's opinion of the value and importance of his requirements now, the easier he will find it to explain the price when he comes to it.

The technique he uses to prehandle the future price objection is, again, the assumptive statement or question by which he transfers to the customer some part of his opinion of value and importance. He has many possible approaches:

> "It must be worth a great deal to you just to know that your policy is one you can rely on?"

> "If we did only this for you, it would pay for the machine on its own, wouldn't it?"

> "From what you tell me, the problem has become so important to you that it is no longer worthwhile trying to find the cheapest way to solve it?"

> "From what you have said, there is nothing cheap about a machine that is so unreliable that you have to throw it away six months after buying it. Reliability is worth something, isn't it?"

Prehandling price in this way reduces its effect as a final objection in absolute terms. However, price is also comparative. If the salesman knows he will face price competition from other companies, he must convince the customer, while he's establishing his decision criteria, that the additional benefits his product offers are important, and that they are well worth buying. Then, when he comes to discuss price in the final stages of the sale, he will show how the additional price of his product is more than compensated for by the additional value that it gives.

If your product costs more, and you can sincerely offer no compensating benefits *at all*, the time has come to review the purpose of your proposition.

Objections based on the new set of circumstances the customer will face if he buys the new product

When the customer changes from one product or system to another, he knows he will face a number of additional problems related to the change. Obviously, some of these problems could be of major importance and will require his special consideration in the negotiation. Many, however, will be of minor significance and will only complicate the decision.

The salesman cannot overcome these problems by shutting his eyes to them. Even if the customer fails to spot them before he signs the order, he will discover them during installation or, worse, when the new system goes into operation. Then, if the problems are major, he will rightly feel the salesman has misled him, and accusations of misrepresentation will begin to fly. *If the problems are major and either cannot be handled after the order has been signed or are likely to be identified by the customer during the negotiation, they must be prehandled now.*

If the salesman handles *minor* problems at the right time, they are insignificant and cause no upset. If the customer discovers them for himself, however, he is likely to react badly to the new problems and find the excuse to reserve his decision:

> "I had not realized this. I'd like to take a day or two to consider my decision."

Here the salesman has needlessly provided the customer with an opportunity to opt out of his decision. In addition, the customer, having found one new problem, will suspect that the salesman has not told him the whole truth at a time when trust is essential for successful negotiation.

The salesman must therefore confront both the major and the minor objections that could arise from the use of the new product while he can control them. The important point to remember is that, if he himself introduces them into the negotiation, he not only gains the customer's respect for his frankness, but also controls the discussion that will take place about them. A word of warning, though: the salesman is not being asked to bare his soul to the customer and introduce unwarranted fears. *He must use his judgment in bringing forward only those objections that could prejudice the success of his sale if they are not handled at this stage.*

The technique for prehandling objections in this category is to be assumptive and matter of fact:

> "We'll have to modify the racking in these trucks and respray them according to the new color scheme and trim, but this should cause no problems. It will make little difference to the average cost per truck."

Here the salesman has frankly admitted to the customer two objections to his product which he could not have avoided, but he has effectively made them part and parcel of the same decision. The customer assumes that they are part of the same decision and will not be able to say later in the sale:

> "Hey, you never told me about that."

Similarly:

> "Of course, being a high-powered car, it's going to use more gasoline, but then you'll get the kind of performance you're looking for."

If gasoline costs are going to be a problem, the customer will ask for the miles per gallon now, before the negotiation continues. The salesman has met his obligation to bring forward the question of gasoline costs, and he can handle this simple objection now quite easily. If the customer does not respond with another question, the salesman does not have to pursue the point and risk frightening him with the actual figures. Logically, anyway, there is no alternative available to the customer, and the salesman points this out:

> "A high-powered car is going to use more gasoline, but that would be true whichever high-powered car you bought."

The approach that appeals to logic is well used whether the objection is of major or minor importance:

> "Of course, any new car you have is bound to require a careful break-in and some routine mechanical adjustments."

8 Handling Competition

To recap, there are three types of competition facing the salesman:

- The customer's natural inertia and desire to do nothing.
- The customer's alternative to spend his money on something entirely different.
- The customer's alternative to buy a directly competitive product or system.

The first two categories of competition—inertia and the multitude of claims on the customer's money—are prehandled by the salesman as he establishes the criteria for ordering. During this time, he shows the customer how important and valuable his immediate decision will be.

The third category of competition—the variety of products in the same class available to the customer—is now prehandled separately.

The first rule in selling against competition is: *Know everything there is to know about competitive products and companies.* Only then can you understand their advantages and disadvantages.

The second rule is: *Never mention your competitors by name.* You are only giving them free advertising, and they are just as easy to talk about in terms of the generic category or product they offer.

The third rule is: *Never knock your competitors,* even if they have been saying nasty things about you and your product. That can only lose you the order, and never wins it.

In this context, remember that the system the customer already has is in competition with your product. The *no knocking* rule applies. The customer may not like what he has, but deep down he will still believe he made a right decision. Don't join in with him if he complains about what he has. Just say:

> "I know what you mean. However, when you chose this product, it was the best on the market. Now there is something better."

There is no need to mention even the possibility of competition if you feel the customer intends to look no further than your product. It can only present an alternative to your product and an excuse to delay the decision.

One way to find out what the customer intends to do is to ask him a question:

> "What are your plans for solving these problems?"

The skill in selling against active competition is the skill in establishing decision criteria with the customer which the competitive products cannot satisfy (see the section "Establishing the Criteria for Ordering" in Chapter 6). If this is done successfully, and the customer suggests the possibility of a competitive product, the salesman can point to the important decision criteria which this product cannot satisfy:

> "This is certainly a very nice product, and in some areas it gives us good competition. Unfortunately, it will not give you all the things you are looking for; specifically. . . . "

In fact, if he has carried out his preparatory work satisfactorily, the salesman can afford to compliment his competition, taking care not to introduce any new factors the customer might be interested in—particularly those benefits the competitors provide that are neither important nor relevant to the customer. Such generosity on the salesman's part will tend ultimately to emphasize the appropriateness of the benefits his product is offering.

If the customer breaks into the negotiation at any stage with a comment about some particular characteristic of a competitive product, the salesman must ask:

> "Why do you think that would be important to you?"

He can then detail all the disadvantages that go with that one competitive advantage, and compare the resulting picture with all the advantages his product offers despite this one disadvantage. In other words, he can outweigh it.

If he knows that the competitive product under consideration is cheaper than his own product, he will have to be successful in impressing on the customer the value and importance of the requirements his product can satisfy.

If, on the other hand, his product costs less and gives less, he will have to show why the additional advantages of the competitive product are just not worth paying for.

As a last resort, he can point out to the customer that, all things considered, he really has only Hobson's choice of first best.

Sometimes, even when the customer has not mentioned competition, the salesman may decide it is safe and worthwhile to bring it up himself in the hope that he will be able to exclude it completely from further consideration and so expedite the decision.

He does this by talking about the competition in generic terms, rather than using specific trade names, and by effectively showing for each category of competition how the disadvantages outweigh the advantages. Any questions the customer now asks are handled individually.

"Basically, the competing vehicle-washing systems fall into three categories: the high-pressure hoses, the spray arches, and the brush machines. The high-pressure hoses work by knocking the dirt off the vehicle, and they do it well and reliably (that is, *pay the highest compliment to the least likely contender*). The trouble with this type of system is that it is hand operated and would be impossible to use with a fleet your size. The spray-arch systems are chemical systems, and are used by firms that run vehicles of a variety of shapes and sizes. The vehicle stands still while the arch traverses its length, spraying it with a chemical detergent. The real advantage of this system is that it does no damage, and it washes off the water-soluble dirt. Unfortunately, it does not wash the front or the back of the vehicle, and the back of the vehicle—and the machine itself— suffers badly from rusting and freezing. Also, vehicles washed in these systems have to be hand washed at least once a week if they are to be kept anything like clean. Finally, there are the revolving-brush systems, which you may have seen in bus depots. They are at their best where there are huge fleets of same-size vehicles. Otherwise they tend to be expensive to buy and costly to maintain and operate. Usually they do not wash the front, back, or roof of the vehicle, and unless they are very carefully used, the heavy revolving brushes can do terrible damage to the paintwork and fittings like mirrors, windshield wipers, and lights."

Having prehandled competition, the salesman is now prepared to move to Stage 2 of the sale and introduce in detail his product and all its benefits. Naturally, not only will his product match the customer's criteria for ordering, but it will also have none of the disadvantages of competitive products.

9 Summarizing for Agreement

Summarizing as a sales technique

The technique of summarizing is basic to any form of persuasion and, therefore, to any form of negotiation.

Summarizing is used in *getting information:*

> "If I may now recap, your present situation is that. . . . "

Summarizing is used in *establishing the criteria for ordering:*

> "From what you have told me, these are the requirements you are seeking to satisfy in the new product: first. . . . "

Later in the sale, summarizing is used in *selling benefits:*

> "We have now seen that the product will satisfy your requirements in the following ways: . . . . "

Still later, summarizing is used in *overcoming objections:*

> "Do I understand correctly that what you are saying is . . . ?"

The whole point of summarizing is to establish agreement between the two parties to the negotiation. Only when agreement has been established at each step in the sale is the salesman safe to go on to the next step. Finally, a question confirms that the summary has been reached.

> "Are you happy with that as a summary of this part of our discussions?"

The summary therefore effectively draws a line under the step in the sale that has been summarized. The implications of that step have been fully explored and agreed upon, and there will be no need to go back over the same ground. If the negotiation begins to flounder in the next step of the sale, either party need only go back to the previous summary and agreement to reestablish a point of reference.

The summary should therefore be used at any point in the sale when a major item in the negotiation has been concluded and agreed upon. The summary confirms mutual understanding, and it confirms agreement.

The *trial close* (see the section "The Trial Close to Establish Commitment" in Chapter 6) fits naturally with the summary of the step in which the salesman develops the implications of the agreement reached in order to establish commitment on the part of the customer.

Also, during the summary of the criteria for ordering, the salesman uses the trial close to confirm the customer's decision criteria as the basis for negotiation and to commit him to a decision based on the satisfaction of these criteria:

> "*If I* could show you that my product satisfies these criteria, *would you* be prepared to place your order for it?"

Similarly, he will use the trial close while *overcoming objections* to establish the importance and relevance of the objection:

> "*If I* could satisfy you on this point, *would you* be prepared to place your order?"

Summarizing is vital in the sale to confirm understanding and to establish agreement. The trial close following the summary is often the logical extension of the summarizing technique.

The salesman's tasks of writing letters and providing quotations are two other means by which he summarizes progress already made. These are discussed in the next two sections.

The letter

Generally no letter need be longer than one page. If it is longer, it usually needs rewriting. You should not expect to hold the attention of a busy man for longer.

In business, all letters must be typed, neatly and cleanly. They must be correctly spelled, paragraphed, punctuated, and dated. There is little excuse for pen or pencil unless it is used to emphasize a point in the letter. You are judged by the appearance of your presentation.

Always answer letters promptly. Before you write, however, ask yourself whether it would be better to answer by telephone or to arrange a meeting, particularly where full understanding is crucial.

Remember that your written communication will remain with you longer than the person to whom you are writing. It may be sitting there in judgment on you a year later.

So make sure you stay close to the truth. Never lie. Never lie on paper, for that is irrefutable evidence. Whenever you think there could be any doubt about your statement, do not say it. Though you may feel you have a reason to say it, do not write it down on paper, ever. The war you are trying to win is the order.

On the other hand, remember that a man who works for a company must file your letter. It may sit there in judgment on his performance too.

With this in mind, do not go further in restating what has actually happened in the negotiation than the position you have already reached. Otherwise, you will be breaking a basic rule in the game, and the customer will be free to find another player.

Written communication falls into three categories: letters, mailshots, and quotations.

Mailshots are used to achieve a specific marketing purpose (see Chapter 4), though in form they should follow the rules for letters. Quotations are discussed in the next section, though they may be accompanied by a covering letter which is, in effect, a *with compliments* slip.

Letters in selling are used to confirm. They confirm an action intended or undertaken, an appointment set, or an agreement made.

You should confirm in writing an important meeting or a demonstration. Similarly, you should confirm in writing an important commitment the customer has made to you or an important action you intend to take.

A letter should be used to consolidate the progress of the sale and establish in writing the position the negotiation has reached. It keeps your proposition in the customer's in-tray and commits him to action.

A letter can improve the wording of your proposition and give the customer a chance for further thought. Besides, letters look trustworthy and add to customer confidence.

All letters must have a specific objective. Otherwise they waste the time of the reader, the writer, and the typist.

In selling, all letters must be brief and direct. Extra words can only damage. Make your point, state your objective—and sign off.

Always write to somebody. Make sure you have the correct name and address, and address the envelope as though it is the right of no other person to open it. Put the correct title on the letter. People like to see their titles on paper.

If you cannot write to the right person by name, do not write at all. If you write to the wrong person, you will have a devil of a time losing him, even though you may succeed in opening the negotiation. Try cold calling the right person instead.

If you have tried all reasonable ways to obtain a name and failed, your customer obviously has no intention of replying to you. Don't even bother to send a brochure. Your time is too valuable to waste on these customers. If you do not believe that, no one else will.

All sales letters must follow the sales pattern of interest, desire, and close (see the section "The Sales Pattern" in Chapter 2). The close, or objective of the letter, should be stated in the first or second sentence. The final paragraph should restate this objective. The intermediate paragraphs should provide the supporting evidence (*interest*) and the appropriate benefits (*desire*), in that order.

Thus each paragraph should contain a separate thought. The first paragraph should contain the objective of your letter:

> "I would like to invite you to a demonstration of our equipment on Friday, October 19."

The objective should be followed in the second paragraph by a statement of high *interest* which will attract the customer and provide him with a reason to be interested in your proposal:

"A number of companies in the trucking industry are already using our equipment and are finding considerable cost savings."

The third paragraph should concern itself with *desire.* Perhaps it is the great benefit he will derive from your proposal:

"I would expect that we could save you 50 percent of your current expenditure and give you far better results than you are getting at the moment."

The fourth paragraph should conclude the letter: a restatement of the objective of the letter and the *close:*

"I therefore hope you will come to the demonstration. I shall phone you on Monday morning to arrange a time that will be suitable for you."

A sales letter should never contain pricing data unless it is being used as a quotation, in which case the rules for quotation apply. At most, it may contain a statement about price where price can be shown not to be a disadvantage.

Be careful with letters. Do not let them weaken your sales presentation by giving away too much information. The letter will play its part in the sale, but the order comes from face-to-face contact.

The quotation

The one great rule with quotations in selling is to try to avoid writing them. They put all the information in the hands of the customer, together with the initiative for response:

"I'll call you when we have reached a decision."

The customer no longer needs you. Unless you have handled the request for the quotation properly, once you leave the room you may never find your way back there again.

Look at it from this point of view. If you were the customer and wanted to get rid of a salesman without upsetting him, what would you ask him for? A quotation.

Quotations also tend to diminish any competitive advantages you might have had. Quotations are usually compared with other quotations, and the most immediately comparable thing in them is price. Customers, however, buy value, not price, and quotations are a poor medium for making benefits, and therefore value, evident.

A decision based on competitive quotations will tend to go to the company offering the lowest price. This is no way for a salesman to fight price competition.

Consequently, there is only one time at which a quotation is written. That is when the customer himself has agreed to buy your product, but absolutely insists that a written quotation must go, for example, before his Board of Directors for formal approval. Even then, the salesman should first try to take the order on a provisional basis, subject to Board approval (see the section "Six Closing Techniques" in Chapter 13).

It is therefore reasonable that, before you write a quotation, you should require the customer to give you a timetable for his decision. Otherwise, you will be writing quotations for people who are trying to get rid of you. If he cannot give you a date for the final meeting, if he cannot confirm when you telephone him for a final decision, you should not write the quotation. It will get you nowhere.

It is not acceptable for them to argue that they might want your product next year. If they want it then, they can have the quotation then, when the prices will probably be higher. No one has the right to waste your time.

Usually formal quotations are unnecessary. An alternative can be provided in longhand at the time of the *close*. It saves time and does not let the customer break away from the pressure to make a decision immediately at that interview. Price can then be presented in its most attractive form, and the customer participates in the explanation and understands how little the price really is.

In an industry where quotations are the norm, the clever company will provide its salesmen with quotation forms that can be completed on the spot. Then the salesman will not have to run the risk of leaving the room before taking the decision.

The formal quotation should be as brief as possible and to the point. It will generally be longer than a letter, but it must be kept to a length and form that will make it likely to be read.

The formal quotation should follow the rules of the letter and be offered in a presentation folder. It should be made up of a one-page summary and conclusions for the busy chairman, followed by appendixes detailing the evidence.

The first page should state in separate paragraphs the recommendation you are making, a summary of findings, and the action you intend to take.

Each appendix should be brief but comprehensive. In separate paragraphs, it should include a conclusion (*close*), the evidence leading to that conclusion (*interest*), and the advantages the customer will find in accepting that conclusion (*desire*), in that order.

Remember, the questions you leave unanswered will have to wait for the next Board meeting. By then it may have become just too much effort:

> "I'm afraid we didn't manage to fit it into our busy schedule this time, but we intend to include it in October's Board meeting."

Make sure your contact with the Board has your arguments firmly in mind. If he is going to persuade his colleagues, you will need a good salesman. Better, try to attend the meeting yourself.

If the quotation is for one man, try to deliver it by hand. Go through it with him and use the opportunity to *close* for the order. The customer may feel his job requires him to obtain a written quotation, and having received and read it he may be quite happy to sign the order immediately.

When you are asked for a quotation, you must strenuously seek an alternative. If you have to leave the room to prepare a quotation, you reduce the momentum you have built up during your presentation. Once you have made your quotation, you lose most of the initiative. Before you do anything, therefore, you must first obtain your customer's personal commitment to purchase:

> "Before I prepare a quotation for you, are you personally satisfied that your company should purchase this product?"

The general rule is: *Try to get out of writing the quotation.* Then, if you really have to write it, it will be an important part of the decision procedure and there is a sound chance it will convert into an order:

> "Why do you need a quotation? Is there something I have not fully explained that is worrying you?"

There are only so many quotations you have time to prepare and follow up, so make sure they are the worthwhile ones.

Unless you have done your homework properly, unless you have fully understood your customer's reasons for wanting your product, unless you have been able to obtain his agreement that your product will satisfy his requirements, unless you have committed him to action, your quotation will join the others in his already overflowing file cabinet.

Finally, a sales office that shoots off a quotation and a brochure in response to every inquiry is a disaster.

Summarizing to establish decision criteria—a special technique

The technique of summarizing to establish the customer's decision criteria is used by skilled salesmen to short-cut the formal steps of *getting information* and *establishing the criteria for ordering* already described. Its purpose and effect are to speed up the negotiation and increase its momentum by reducing the amount of time between opening the interview and closing it.

The technique itself is assumptive. It assumes, by statements rather than questions, that the customer recognizes his current situation and his unsatisfied requirements; it proposes the criteria that must be satisfied in a decision of this nature; and it seeks the customer's commitment to a decision based on these criteria if the salesman can satisfy them.

It is a confident technique and can really be used only when the salesman feels he is in such a strong competitive position that the only question the customer can dispute is whether he should make his decision now or later.

The dangers in this sales technique are obvious. The formal process for *getting information* and *establishing the criteria for ordering* ensures that the salesman will gather all the necessary information, will understand the customer's own special requirements, and will prehandle any of the basic objections to a decision. His decision to short-cut this process means that he may run into pitfalls he would otherwise have avoided—and any one of them can be fatal. For example, by prescribing a course of action he intends to take rather than agreeing formally with the customer on the most suitable course, the salesman takes the risk that his presentation may be inappropriate. Even the slightest incongruity can lead to dissidence and create objections that would otherwise have been avoided.

Good judgment and the right assessment of the risks involved are important in deciding when this technique should be used. It is therefore a technique that should be used advisedly, and only by a *skilled* salesman.

The framework for this technique is best shown in an example.

S. Good morning, Mr. Chadwick. My name is Lund. I'm the area sales manager for the Wash-Clean Company.

Introduction

C. Good morning, Mr. Lund.

S. We can wash clean any shape or size of vehicle all over in less than three minutes—not only the sides, but the roof, the front, and the back; in fact, every nook and cranny—leaving a high shine and a corrosion-resistant finish.

Claim

C. Really.

S. We have something like three hundred machines installed now with industrial companies, from Gower Bros. in the food trade to Hodder and Co. in the chemical industry, and they are all delighted with it.

Claim substantiated

C. I have heard about you, possibly from the trade papers.

S. I understand from one of your drivers that you have eighty vehicles of your own in this depot, and that three men have considerable problems trying to keep them clean.

Information on which proposal will be made

C. Yes. You can see they do.

S. Mr. Chadwick, if I could show you that our equipment will give you the clean vehicles you want, that the price will be no more than the money you are spending at this moment, and that you have a suitable site to install it, would you be prepared to place your order with us?

The trial close — in fact, this is the first question the salesman has asked

C. Yes. After all this time, we'd really like to solve our vehicle-washing problem.

What more can he say to this reasonable and businesslike proposal?

S. Right. Let's first go into your yard to see *where* it *will* be installed. If there is nowhere to put it, that will be the end of our discussion.

Assumptive technique: the salesman is placing the above equipment before he has sold it.

From the moment the salesman walks onto the site, he will be asking questions designed to fill his bank of vital information.

Using this technique, the salesman has divided his presentation into three objectives: locating the equipment, showing its capability to wash, and agreeing on price. These are the three *sales* he must close to take the order. The latter two objectives he will handle at a demonstration he will make arrangements for when he has concluded his site check. Perhaps, however, he will try to *close* the order during this call, even on a provisional basis, subject to demonstration. He could do this successfully by claiming that the experience of existing satisfied customers provides a more valid proof of capability than a demonstration.

10 Selling Benefits

Relating benefits to product features

Unless he is buying a Rembrandt, a customer buys a product or system for what it will do for him, rather than for what it is—that is, for the benefits it will bring him.

A benefit is an actual advantage the customer will gain from using or owning your product. When a customer details to the salesman the requirements he is seeking to satisfy in his purchasing decision, he expresses himself in benefit terms. For example, he might want a truck-washing machine *that will wash any vehicle commercially clean any time it returns to the depot, without having to employ special labor.*

On the other hand, the salesman's product or system incorporates a number of physical and operational features. For example, his truck-washing machine might have high-speed regenerative pumps and fully pre-programmed electrical circuitry.

Now, in this example, both what the customer wants and what the salesman is offering are the same. Yet if the customer states his requirements as a fast turnaround of clean vehicles through equipment operated by the drivers, and the salesman replies with regenerative pumps and pre-programmed electrical circuitry, all the customer will be able to do is to look him straight back in the eye. He will not understand a word.

The greater the apparent technicality of the product, the greater the chance that the salesman will fall into exactly this trap. He will be overcome by the cleverness of his product and his fund of technical knowledge. He will talk at length all about his regenerative pumps. The customer will nod his head wisely—he does not want to appear a fool. But no understanding, no sale. At the end of the interview the customer will congratulate the salesman and thank him for all his trouble. The salesman will walk out with a smile as big as the doorway, quite convinced that this is the one sale he will make. He won't.

The more technical your product, the closer you must stay to the rule: *People buy a product or service because of the benefits it will bring them, not for what it is.* The salesman's description of product features must therefore be used only to prove the related benefits the customer will gain. The key words the salesman must use are "which means":

> "The high-speed pumps will wash a vehicle in less than three minutes, *which means* that it can be washed any time it returns to the depot. The action of the pump ensures that the dirt is removed and that the vehicle is cleaned to the standard you require. As far as operation is concerned, the machine wash cycle is pre-programmed electrically. *This means* that it can be worked by anyone, night or day. All the driver has to do is park his vehicle in the wash bay, press the one button, and walk away. Three minutes later, the vehicle will be clean and shiny."

The role of the salesman is to show the relation of the features his product is offering to the benefits the customer is seeking. If he has done his groundwork properly, the benefits the customer is seeking will be the same as the ones the salesman has recommended; and the benefits the salesman has recommended will be the ones that match the features of his product.

So the first step, even before you go out to sell, is to make a list of all your product features, beginning with physical characteristics and going on through the operational characteristics. Against each feature, list the related benefits, keeping in mind all the different ways the customers in different industries use your product. What special benefits do they find? The list might look like this:

PRODUCT FEATURE	EXAMPLES OF RELATED BENEFITS
Physical characteristics	
Aluminum wash frame	Will not rust—low maintenance cost
	Good appearance
	Light weight—will install in most existing roof structures

Hoist motor	Light weight of frame means motor operates well within capability
Independent suspension points	No danger from collapse
Plastic pipes	Will not rust or corrode
Stainless steel jets	Will not corrode: long wear life
Filters	Jets seldom block and are easily cleaned
Watertight limit switches	No maintenance requirement
	No damage to vehicles from equipment misuse
Switchable cross-spray systems	Wash any length of vehicle in same wash
	Wash between cab and body
	No danger of vehicle damage
Steel equipment consols	Guts of equipment safe from vehicle collision
Bronze regenerative pumps	Specially designed to pump the chemical formulas without corrosion
	Long wear life; reliable
Automatic chemical system	No wastage from human error
	Ensures correct chemical mixes for effective washing
Programmed electrical circuitry	Single button control
	Anyone can operate it
	No requirement for special labor
	No special labor costs
	Machine can be operated at any time

Operational characteristics

High-speed wash	Fast vehicle turnaround
	Wash any time vehicle returns to depot
	No waiting lines
	More frequent washing reduces damage from road salts
	No need now to have dirty vehicles

Chemical action	No damage from brushes to wipers, mirrors, or trim
	Paint life prolonged
	Vehicle dries with high shine
	Windows dry without smear
	Corrosion inhibitor in chemical increases body life
Design of wash	For the first time, vehicles can be washed all over—sides, front, back, even the roof
	Vehicles look clean rather than *cleaned*
	Good advertising appeal of clean vehicles
	Low maintenance cost
Fully automatic	Anyone can operate it at any time
	No special skills required
	Labor costs saved
	Controlled chemical usage and cost

Note: Extend the list by asking yourself "which means?" after every benefit. Beware of in-house jargon that the customer will not understand.

The customer listed the benefits he is seeking when he established his criteria for ordering. The salesman now shows how his product provides the benefits the customer is seeking by relating these benefits to the physical and operational features of his product. The customer now begins to see the product as the solution to his problem.

Benefit chains

Benefit chains are used by the salesman to develop the full implication of the benefits the customer is seeking and the product is offering. Consequently they increase the meaningfulness of these benefits to the customer and, therefore, his *desire to possess* the product as a solution to his problem. They also reinforce his confidence in his own decision criteria and his willingness to make a decision based on them.

Each product feature has one or more benefits. In turn, each benefit has a logical chain of related benefits. Each link in the chain extends the implication of the previous benefit rather than qualifying the meaning. This *is* important to understand.

Take, for example, a car with a high-powered engine. The high-powered engine is a product feature. *More power* and *fast* are two possible benefits of this feature and can be developed into chains of related benefits:

CAR WITH THE FEATURE OF A HIGH-POWERED ENGINE

Positive benefit chain (1)	*Positive benefit chain (2)*
More power	Fast
Greater passing safety margin	Gets there in half the time
Less strain from driving	Can be used for business as well as pleasure
You can do more when you get there	Better value for money invested

Notice how one benefit leads logically to the next and develops the implication of the previous benefit. (Try putting the words "which means" after each benefit.)

Now for every *positive* benefit chain that represents the situation to be gained, there is a comparable *negative* benefit chain that represents the situation to be avoided. This might be the customer's current system or a method competing with the one the salesman is proposing:

CAR WITHOUT THE FEATURE OF THE HIGH-POWERED ENGINE

Negative benefit chain (1)	*Negative benefit chain (2)*
Insufficient power	Slow
Smaller passing safety margin	Takes forever to get there
More strain from driving	Fit for nonbusiness use only
You're exhausted by the time you get there	Poor value if you are going to spend the money

How does the salesman bring these benefits together?

The salesman talks in benefit terms to describe his product and the actual words he uses relate as far as possible to those the customer used in listing his decision criteria. The benefits he now emphasizes are those that his product offers and those that the customer has specified will satisfy his requirement. As he emphasizes each benefit, he underlines it by simultaneously stressing the comparable negative benefit, or *disbenefit*.

In the case of the high-powered car, the customer is looking for less driving strain after a bad year of highway driving in an underpowered car. The salesman knows that the customer is a businessman who has to travel a great deal in his job. First, he points out that the bigger high-powered engine will use more gasoline. This is an objection he knows he will have to face, and it is better to face it sooner than later. Now he goes through benefit chain 1. He reaches "less strain," compares it with the customer's present situation, and extends the implication:

> ". . . which means you'll feel like doing more when you get there. That's better than arriving exhausted each time, isn't it? Not only that. . . ."

The customer's response encourages him to develop benefit chain 2 and to link "less strain" with "for business as well as pleasure." The words "not only that" introduce the next benefit chain.

The customer's interest increases:

> "Really? Is that right?"

This looks like the product he needs:

> "That's interesting. I hadn't thought of that!"

In this way, the salesman links the benefits the customer is seeking to the features his product is offering, and develops the full implication of the relevance of these features to the customer's needs by making the comparison with the customer's current situation. By the time he has covered all the customer's criteria for ordering in this way, the customer will be enthusiastic about the product as a solution to his problems and therefore willing to go ahead with his decision. Now all the salesman will have to do is to summarize the benefits in preparation for closing the sale.

It is critical in the use of this technique that the customer be forced to express his attitude verbally toward the implication of the benefit chains. Rule: *Never communicate a benefit without a check question.* Particularly if the customer's response is slow, the salesman must ask:

"This is what you wanted, isn't it?"

Or

"What would this mean to you?"

With this commitment, the customer is forced to accept or dispute. If he accepts, his enthusiasm will grow, however gradually. If he disputes, the salesman will know he has to take another tack. Without this commitment, the customer can avoid the decision completely.

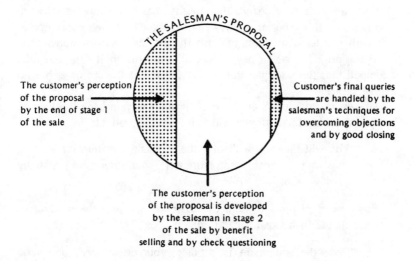

The customer's perception of the proposal by the end of stage 1 of the sale

THE SALESMAN'S PROPOSAL

Customer's final queries are handled by the salesman's techniques for overcoming objections and by good closing

The customer's perception of the proposal is developed by the salesman in stage 2 of the sale by benefit selling and by check questioning

Relating benefits to customer criteria

The customer has listed his criteria for ordering and the salesman has agreed upon a summary of them to make sure there are no misunderstandings or omissions. He then trial closes to obtain commitment to a decision and prehandles the likely objections to the decision. Now he begins benefit selling to prove the relevance of his product features to the customer's needs and to arouse the customer's enthusiasm, and therefore his desire, for the product.

He takes each of the customer's decision criteria in turn, relates it to the relevant product feature, and develops the implication of that feature through benefit chains. Once he has provided the proof, he says:

> "Are you now satisfied that we can handle this side of your problem for you?"

With each "yes" answer, he moves on to the next decision criterion. With any "no" answer, he asks "Why," to establish the exact reason for the negative response, before trying again to establish the proof.

If the "no" proves particularly intractable, leave it until last and continue with each of the other criteria in turn. By the time you come back to it, his resistance to this particular proof may have weakened in the face of the other benefits the product will bring him.

Otherwise the only chance the salesman has is to show that the importance of this criterion is anyway outweighed by the importance of the other criteria, in terms of both the job the customer wants done and the price he has to pay. Depending on his ability to prehandle competition, the salesman might also show that the customer has no other choice.

Use the words "you" and "your" prominently in benefit selling to emphasize what the customer will gain from the product:

> "*You* will find *you* will solve the problem of equipment freezing up in the winter and, moreover, *your* drivers will actually enjoy using it."

Paint word pictures to help the customer visualize the product or service in use in his own operation:

> "Once the equipment is installed, your drivers need only stop their vehicles in the wash bay, press the button, and walk away. In three minutes, the vehicle will be bright, shining, and clean, and all they'll have to do is pick it up."

Emphasize value whenever possible to reduce the impact of the price announcement and to increase the urgency of the decision:

> "With this equipment installed, not only will you save the cost of bodywork damage, but your customers, when they see your shining clean vehicles, will say 'Here's a company that runs its business properly.'"

Be enthusiastic about your product. If you are not, no one else is going to be. But do not exaggerate claims unless you can meet them. While enthusiasm will increase your credibility, exaggeration will decrease it.

Exaggerated claims you cannot meet will only return to haunt you after the sale is made. A customer will accept a product's deficiencies as long as it also does what he wants it to do. He will never accept a product that does not reach the claims made for it by the salesman, whether these claims are relevant to his situation or not.

The claims you make for your product influence the customer's expectation of it. If you can still achieve your objective, it is almost better to understate your claims and let the customer find out for himself that your product is even better than you described it.

Do not get too involved in technical detail. The salesman need only know enough technical information to answer the questions of the man he is selling to. Technical evidence should be used only to prove a related benefit. Otherwise, it is likely only to confuse.

Once the technical discussion goes beyond the point of proving benefits, the chances are that the sale is moving off course. The salesman must close down this line of conversation before he loses control, even if he knows the answer:

> "I'm really not an expert on pumps. I probably know a great deal less about them than you. All I can say is that they will not be corroded by the chemicals and that they operate well within their capacity. Their guaranteed work life is two years, and they should last at least twice as long as this."

Once you have stressed the features and benefits of the product that satisfy the customer's criteria for ordering, mention briefly the other great advantages the product will bring him. The benefits that satisfy the criteria for ordering are what he is buying—the other advantages he gets for free. However, they can be the icing on the cake, and they relay the impression that, all in all, the product is very *inexpensive* for the great variety of things it offers.

Mention them only briefly, though. You cannot do more than sell. Once you have satisfied the criteria for ordering, you have really done enough to ask for the order. Extra talking, therefore, is likely to prejudice your chances of success.

Use judgment. Keep your talking down to what is necessary. And remember, you are there to solve his problems, not to boast about your product.

Once you have shown that the features of your product match the customer's decision criteria, and you have his agreement in each case that this is so, *summarize*. Use a pen and paper if they will help:

> "Good. If I may now summarize: you said that, in buying a new truck-washing facility, you wanted equipment that would give you A, B, and C. You've agreed that our equipment can give you A, B, and C because of its features 1, 2, and 3, and besides all that, it gives you benefits D, E, and F. Are you now happy that our equipment can satisfy your requirements?"

If you initially established his criteria for ordering properly, he can only say yes. If he says no, ask: "Why not?" The customer will now detail those areas about which he is not quite happy, and, if necessary, the salesman will check for understanding with a question:

> "Why do you mention this especially?"

Or

> "What exactly do you mean by this?"

With this understanding, the salesman will then answer the new question with reference to the benefits of his product:

> S. Now are you happy that our equipment can satisfy your requirements?
> C. Yes.

Now *close:*

> "Shall we therefore go ahead with your order?"

The customer has several alternatives. He can:

> — Ask to see it first.

— Ask for a written quotation.
— Try to put off the decision with an insincere objection.
— Make a sincere objection.
— Say he is going to buy a competitor's product.
— Ask how much it costs.
— Say yes if he already knows how much it costs.

The demonstration

All products, whatever they are, must be demonstrated in the sale. Even service products must be demonstrated. For example, the death notices in the newspaper are a good demonstration of the need for life insurance: people do die. It is almost a paradox, but it's true—*the more difficult the product is to demonstrate, the more important it is that a successful demonstration be made.*

Demonstrations are made in two ways: through visual aids and by formal site demonstrations. Visual aids are discussed in the next section.

Most salesmen who use formal site demonstrations will also use visual aids. Ideally it is better to complete the sale using visual aids, because it makes a further meeting at the demonstration site unnecessary. However, site demonstrations are important, and because they are so visual, they tend to be *effective*. A salesman who knows he must demonstrate this way to sell his product will often begin his negotiation at the demonstration site, in order to cut out the first call.

Demonstrations prove the benefits of a product. The salesman accentuates these benefits by making them visual and therefore increasing the customer's desire to own them.

The customer comes to a demonstration to gain confidence in his decision and to ascertain that the product is *capable* of doing the job the salesman described. This is important to remember. Although it is desirable, it is not vital that the product perform well during demonstration. This could have been *fixed*. It is vital, however, that the salesman be able to persuade the customer that the product will perform well in practice.

Demonstrations are basically concerned with selling benefits. However, because they have a high interest factor, they are also used for obtaining the interview and for bringing forward long-term prospective customers:

> "We're visiting your area on Tuesday to demonstrate our equipment to the Macmillan Company. We'd also like to show it to you. Would 2:00 P.M. be suitable for you, or would 4:30 P.M. be more convenient?" (*Alternative close*)

Or

> "You may remember we talked together about six months ago. We are holding a demonstration of our new equipment at the Macmillan Company on Tuesday, June 1st, and we'd like you to come along. Would 2:00 P.M. be suitable for you, or would 4:30 P.M. be more convenient?" (*Alternative close*)

If your product requires demonstration to be sold, it is generally not worthwhile arranging to call on the customer beforehand. Usually this call is redundant and can even reduce the customer's interest in coming to the demonstration. It is better, therefore, to make the demonstration the first call and arrange the appointment by telephone.

The exception is where you discover the customer by a cold call. In this case, you can arrange the demonstration as the second call and use the cold call to introduce the concept of the product and to carry out site checks. Obviously, as you will always try to *close* for the order at any call you make, you will try to close the order across the table during the cold call and perhaps let the customer escape an immediate decision by offering him the demonstration.

No one will buy your product just because you can prove it is a good one. They will buy it only if they believe that it will provide them with a satisfactory solution to their problem. Before you can demonstrate, you must find out what this problem is.

Always establish an objective for the demonstration. When you have achieved it, *close* it. Unless you close it, you can never be quite sure that the customer has agreed that you have achieved it.

The objective for the demonstration could be established in this way:

> "I want to show you that this product will do what we have agreed you need."

The close for this demonstration would therefore be:

> "Are you now happy that this product will do what we have agreed you need?"

Another objective for the demonstration could be established by a question:

> "*If I* can show you that the product will do the things you say you want, *will you* place your order with me?"

The close for this demonstration would therefore be:

> "You've agreed that the product will do the things you say you want. Shall we now go ahead and place your order?"

The demonstration should go on only long enough for you to achieve your objective. Once you have achieved it, you should finish the demonstration. There is nothing left for you to demonstrate.

If the customer insists that you go on with your demonstration after you consider you have achieved your objective, the simple point is that you have not achieved it. The customer must still have a remaining question. You should therefore treat it as any other question, understand exactly *what* he wants to find out *and why*, and then provide the satisfactory answer.

You should use only as much information as you need to close the demonstration. More information than the customer requires can only raise new questions, and possibly new fears.

The purpose of any demonstration is to show that the product has the capability to do what you say it will do. Any likelihood that the product will fail during demonstration represents an objection that should be prehandled:

> "This equipment has not been especially prepared for demonstration. We want you to see how it performs under normal operating conditions. Like any other machine, it could break down. What I want you to understand, however, is that it has the capability of doing the job you want. Is that O.K.?"

If the product collapses during demonstration, don't give up. Explain to the customer, quite reasonably, that this can happen with any product, and tell him what your company does in such a circumstance. Then go on with your demonstration, even if all you can do is wave your arms in the air. There is no real reason why you should not still be able to achieve the purpose of your demonstration.

Demonstrations at existing customers' premises add credibility to the product. The prospective buyer can see how naturally your product fits into operational conditions, and he can talk to your customer about the problems and advantages he finds in his new situation. This helps the prospective buyer overcome his reluctance to make a change.

When you use existing customers' premises, make sure first that you can have confidence in your contact there. Obviously, he can make or mar your sale. Even talk to him first about the kinds of benefit the prospective customer is looking for and the points you would like him to emphasize. Then, if you have confidence in him, don't worry about the way he presents your product. He is going to say good and bad things about it, but he will make sure that the arguments are weighted in your favor. Your interruptions will only detract from his presentation; so why not go for a walk and try to leave them alone for a while?

Demonstrations can be particularly effective on the prospective customer's own premises where he and his staff can practice with it and actually see it in operation. In this situation, it is usually desirable to demonstrate a unit you can leave behind *on trial*. This course could make the customer's decision easier.

At the demonstration, make sure everyone who has to see the product sees it. One demonstration is enough. More than one is wasting time, and it weakens your control over the decision timetable.

Confirm the appointment by letter, giving date, time, and place. Telephone to confirm the appointment on the day of the demonstration.

Organize your presentation beforehand. Make sure you have everyone and everything you need.

Welcome your customer and thank him for coming. Sit him down with a cup of coffee. Agree with him on the objectives of the demonstration. Trial close him:

> "*If* the product can do the things we have agreed on, *will you* be prepared to place your order for it?"

He will probably laugh and say:

"Show me first."

But you have moved him mentally. He knows you are asking for the order and you expect a decision from him. It brings him up to the starting line.

At this stage, it is always worthwhile to ask for a decision if the demonstration is successful, and even to make an issue out of it. Why should he have the chance to go away and think about it? Why can't he make a decision right away when the decision is obvious? Insist on your right for a decision. Put pressure on him to commit himself. After all, if he is not prepared to consider the decision, the demonstration itself is really pointless.

In demonstrating to a group, demonstrate to the man making the decision without showing lack of interest in his colleagues. If you think one of his subordinates is going to throw out objections, make sure you have someone from your side to talk to him in another part of the room. He probably only wants attention anyway.

If you have no such help, choose your moment and put the trouble-maker down firmly but not rudely. You will have the sympathy of his colleagues. You will make him consider his future questions more carefully. And having put him down, address part of the demonstration to him as though in answer to his questions. Show that you care about him and his opinion. Discipline and love travel well together.

In demonstrating equipment, begin by demonstrating the physical features before going on to the operational features. *Never demonstrate a product feature without demonstrating the related benefit as well.*

Sell the magic of a machine. People respond to a machine, particularly if it moves. Become adept at its operation and make it move in time with your demonstration. Give it the chance to sell itself. Be quiet while it is operating. Do not attract attention away from it by talking too much.

Scripted demonstrations are well worth learning. Even when they are parrotlike, they are more than usually effective. They will hold the important benefits in your mind when you come under pressure, and they match your talking to the movement of the machine, to give benefit to both.

Do not be distracted by questions. They quickly multiply. Unless the question is particularly thorny, ask if you can take it later, and answer it then, when it is worth trying to see whether it has been forgotten.

Let the customer use the product himself. He will enjoy participating, and it helps him to see himself using it in the future.

You should do what is reasonable to achieve the objectives of the demonstration, as agreed upon during the initial discussion, and no more. You will not win the order by running additional errands for the customer. You should not, for example, use his samples unless they are special to his situation. They can only be a distraction. They could go wrong, and if they do, you might lose control.

It is too easy to become involved in the paraphernalia of a sale and the areas of distraction that lie around them. It is too easy to lose sight of the objective of the demonstration, particularly if the customer becomes excited by your product. The customer will try to sidetrack you. This is another way he takes the pressure off himself. You must resist him successfully. The penalty is losing the order.

Do not misuse the demonstration. Never make the product do more than it is meant to do. Do not take unnecessary risks. It cannot help the sale; and, if it fails, you could lose the order.

Confirm what you have achieved in the demonstration with questions to obtain agreement. Make sure the customer understands the implication of the steps as you take them. Keep the demonstration tight, and you will keep the interest high.

If the equipment breaks down, go on with the demonstration. Use third-party references to confirm that it does work well in practice. Convince the customer of the product's potential to perform the function; there then should be no further need for demonstration.

If the product starts doing terrible things, it is better to walk the customer out of the room so that he does not see the dimensions of the disaster. In many cases, however, it is possible to wander off to another piece of equipment as though nothing has happened. If you are working in a showroom, rapport with the showroom girl can cover these possibilities.

If you are demonstrating on the prospective customer's premises and you want to leave equipment on trial, never leave it on free trial. "Free" means "no commitment," and you are selling commitment.

A demonstration is an emotional high point in the sale. It therefore cannot be completed until you *close* for the order. It must be constructed in such a way that the logical ending is the request for the order. It must have a beginning, a middle, and an end. It must be closed.

In reality, demonstrations as a second call are logically meaningless as far as proving capability is concerned. If the product performs too well, the customer will only think you have *doctored* it. And if it performs badly, it is not necessarily going to perform badly in practice. The fact that you have so many famous customers using your product so happily is really better evidence.

With this argument firmly in your mind, there is no logical reason why you should not be able to take the order across the table at an interview in the customer's office, at least on a provisional basis subject to demonstration. Then, if you can do this, there is always the chance that the customer might just decide that it is not worth wasting valuable time at the demonstration, and telephone you for an immediate delivery.

Visual aids

Whether you are a company chairman selling to another company chairman, or a husband selling to a wife, you must use visual aids if you want to persuade effectively.

Visual aids are essential in any form of selling. No good salesman would risk selling without them. They fulfill three important functions:

- They hold interest because they are visual.
- They reduce the chance of misunderstanding by visually confirming meaning.
- They allow the sales message to be presented through the eyes as well as through the ears. Two of the five senses are activated—this, after all, is what makes television such an effective advertising medium.

The great problem with visual aids, and the reason why most people do not use them, is that they take a little time and thought to prepare. It is always easier to neglect this elementary preparation in selling, and it is often fatal. Preparing visual aids is a matter of discipline.

Every product and service has visual representation. For a product, it can be pictures or line drawings of the product by itself or in operational conditions. This type of visual aid is normally held in a folder with the inserts in clear acetate panels in a sequence to match the sales presentation. In equipment selling, this sequence should match the one used in the demonstration. Alternatively, the visual aid can be a letter from a satisfied customer.

For a service, the visual aid can be pictures of what things were like before the service was taken and, for comparison, pictures showing the advantages the service brings.

One of the great differences between selling a product and selling a service is that, with a product, you have something concrete to demonstrate, whereas a service is abstract and therefore without physical definition. Either way, however, the customer still buys the same thing—namely, what the product or service will do for him.

One of the keys to selling a service is to create the form of visual aid that will emphasize the difference between having and not having the service. For example, *cleanliness* is just a concept, but pictures can give it reality by showing something that is clean and something that is dirty. Similarly, insurance company bonus records can be shown graphically, and money can be shown as what it will buy.

Visual aids are not the only visual forms the salesman has available. He can paint word pictures by helping the customer to visualize what life will be like when the new product is installed. He can use his hands to emphasize points that require emphasis, and to describe the shape or actions of products he is describing. He can use a pencil and paper to draw descriptive pictures, or to make important figures and numbers a reality, perhaps by showing the comparison between proposed and existing methods.

Visual aids can be desk film shows that run the risk of turning your customer into an amateur film critic.

Visual aids can also be machines the customer operates, or products he is allowed to handle. Samples are important visual aids, and care should be taken to see that they are attractively finished and packaged.

Some products, particularly those that are the raw material of another manufacturing operation, are sold for the service they provide, such as low wastage, low machine wear, fast delivery, and service support. Visual aids devised for these products must emphasize these benefits.

Never use a brochure as a visual aid. Otherwise the customer is likely to shorten your presentation by telling you to leave the brochure and that he will telephone you *if* he is interested.

When you use visual aids, make sure your customer is seated so that he can see them comfortably. Since they tend to create interest, make sure also that only one item is presented for his interest at a time, and do not leave the ones you have already used lying around to distract him. Similarly, if you are presenting visual aids to a group of people, it is important that they should all be able to see and discuss the same visual aid item at the same time.

Make the way you present your product vivid and exciting but don't appear to be putting on an act. Similarly, present your product forcibly, but not overbearingly.

Third-party references

The first sale for a new product in any market is the most difficult. The customer must be made to decide on an unknown product from an untried supplier, just at the time when the salesman's own presentation is weakest because he himself is new to the product. It is for this very reason that most companies are prepared to negotiate especially advantageous terms for the first customers of their new product.

How much easier it is to sell when you can show the customer a list of well-known companies that use your product, and can describe the ways in which companies in the customer's particular business use it. It must bring confidence and authority to the sale, and this makes the customer's decision easier.

Third-party references give your new customer the assurance that other good companies have made the same decision before him. This is why third-party references should be used liberally throughout the sale. After all, he will reason, they cannot all be fools.

An enthusiastic letter from a satisfied customer will confirm this confidence. Check with the customer first that the letter may be used. He is unlikely to refuse this sudden fame. Properly used, the letter can save you a call or the need for a demonstration.

Most existing customers can be used as third-party references, even when your product has not behaved particularly well for them. They are unlikely to discredit their own decision, and there is always something good they can say about the new method.

So make a list of your customers and call on each of them personally, to make sure they are happy with you. Break this list down by industry, by product usage, and by geographical area.

The only time a customer will discredit your product is when he feels you have neglected him or left him to fend for himself in times of trouble. Customer neglect carries a considerable risk—no sale is over when the order is taken.

Most prospective customers will not bother to contact existing customers for advice. Names will be sufficient. If they want to telephone, make sure they telephone the customers you have prepared for this possibility. You can influence this by providing specific contact names and telephone numbers.

In using a third-party reference, make sure you do not give the customer the excuse to put his decision off to another day while he makes his inquiry. Insist that he telephone immediately, and keep the pressure on him to make a decision.

A third-party reference has a number of other functions in the sale besides winning the customer's confidence. For example, it can be used to prehandle the objection that the customer's problem is unique. It can be used to handle main objections to the product, on the basis either that other customers do not experience the problems or that they find these comparatively minor problems are by far outweighed by the real advantages of the product.

A third-party reference is also a good way to insinuate an overwhelming benefit in order to build its effect. The customer cannot know all the benefits of your product, and you dilute their effect if you offer them in a flood. So scatter some around where he is likely to find them. How much greater the impact is when he thinks he has discovered an important advantage for himself.

Say nothing about one customer to another except those things you would not mind his hearing. It is a good motto for living too.

It is difficult to sell without third-party references. And it is silly not to make full use of them when you are fortunate enough to have them. Make sure you spell them out.

11 Overcoming Objections

Objections as signposts in the sale

The customer asks questions and gives opinions throughout the sales negotiation. The salesman checks for understanding, answers the questions, modifies the customer's opinion, and gains the agreement that suits his presentation.

While he is establishing the customer's criteria for ordering, the salesman as far as possible prehandles the objections he feels he is likely to meet later in the sale. He then shows that the benefits of his product match the customer's requirements. Now he summarizes, agrees on the match, and *closes* for the order on the basis of this agreement:

"Shall we therefore go ahead with the order?"

A customer's yes brings the negotiation to its conclusion and the order is placed. A customer's no indicates the first objection to which the salesman replies:

"Why not? What is troubling you?"

In selling, *why* is the key word for understanding the meaning and the reason for the objection:

"*Why* do you say that?"

"*Why* is that?"

"*Why*?"

Obviously, understanding the reason for the objection is as important as understanding its meaning. Before he answers this objection, the salesman might also ask:

"Are there any other problems?"

A customer's yes is followed by the salesman's question:

"What are they, and why are they a problem to you?"

The salesman will then see the ground he has yet to cover before he can take the order.

A customer's no followed by a trial close will bring the end of the negotiation in sight:

C. No. That is the only problem.
S. *If I* can solve this problem for you, *then will you* be happy to place your order?

Objections at this stage of the sale point to the route the salesman must take to win the order. As the objections are overcome, so are the reasons against the purchase. Theoretically, at least, once you have overcome the customer's final objection, there is no possible reason why he should not place his order with you immediately.

If the customer has any interest in your product, he is almost bound to question the details of its suitability to his own particular situation. He is seeking an optimum solution to his problem, and this must lie somewhere in the balance of advantages and disadvantages of your product. It is perfectly natural that he should question his understanding of this balance to consolidate his own decision. The salesman, therefore, should understand clearly the role of objections in his presentation and make sure he turns them to his advantage.

No professionally trained salesman has ever taken a sales course and not heard about the mystical *buying signal.* In fact, the buying signal is no more than the customer's bringing forward familiar terminal questions such as these:

"How should I pay for it?"

"When can delivery be made?"

"Do you think the blue one is best?"

Properly answered, these questions will serve only as requests for further information; but the salesman must be careful! Wrong answers will introduce new attitudes around which fully fledged objections will harden.

Quite often, these questions come earlier than the salesman has planned that they would in his presentation. They mean that the customer is already looking through his final objections to purchasing. The salesman has done what he has needed to do in his presentation. He must therefore cut short whatever he has left to say and switch immediately to the step for handling objections in preparation for the *close*. The sale negotiation will change now in character from presentation to a sequence of customer questions and salesman answers. Once the customer has the information he requires for his decision, the salesman will *close* finally for the order. If the customer now fails to *sign*, the salesman can still return to the point where he left his presentation, and continue with the sale.

Sincere and insincere objections

In selling, some objections are sincere and some are insincere. It is obviously important to be able to distinguish between them. Otherwise, the negotiation will disintegrate as you set off in chase of the phantom rabbits. Once the customer gets you sincerely answering his insincere objections, he will lead you down a path along which, like Sir Thomas More, you will never return.

However, it is also true that sometimes the customer will present insincere objections which effectively cover his sincere objections. The salesman can therefore never afford to treat an objection casually. He must find his way through these distractions to the real questions the customer wants to ask. The only way he will do this is by being reasonable and thorough.

The technique for testing whether an objection is sincere or insincere is to *trial close* it. You trial close only when you know you understand the meaning and reason for the objection:

> "*If (suppose) I* could solve this problem you mention, *would you* order my product?"

If the customer says yes, then his objection was sincere. If he goes straight on to another objection, then his first objection was insincere and not worth answering. He does not want an answer.

If the customer continues to give you insincere objections and fails to respond to the challenge of the trial close, you must challenge him directly with words such as these:

> "You've mentioned a number of things that are on your mind, but, when I've asked you if these are seriously affecting your ability to make a decision, you've gone on to something else. What real obstruction is there to prevent you doing business with us?"

If you are unable to get through to the final objection, you will never sell. And if you are worried about having to be so forceful, remember that you cannot lose an order you have not got.

If the customer bombards you with insincere objections, and shows an intention to continue talking, let him talk himself to a standstill. Just sit there and look at him. Then, when he has stopped, ask him what the real reason is for his hesitancy. Whatever you do, do not let him draw you into an argument. That you will always lose.

If the customer exaggerates his objection, restate the objection without the exaggeration, gain his agreement that you are still talking about the same thing, and answer it if it still needs answering.

Whether the objection is sincere or insincere, never categorically tell the customer (or, for that matter, anyone) that he is wrong to think the way he does, because maybe he does not believe he is, and communication will be lost. If you just have to say something, say it in question form:

> "In some ways you are probably right, but do you think in this instance the evidence could point to this conclusion . . . ?"

Sincere objections involve a real desire for additional information, and this desire either is expressed or just sits silently in the customer's mind troubling him. The full meaning of sincere objections must be made explicit with questions, both to gain understanding and to ensure that silent objections are voiced.

Overcoming emotional and facetious objections

Emotional objections are related to hesitancy in making a decision, desire to avoid a decision, prejudice, or sheer cussedness.

People are resistant to change because of:

- Risk: *Better the devil you know. . . .*
- Inconvenience from the disruption caused by the change.
- Satisfaction with present conditions: *It does a very good job, even though yours does better.*
- Fear of criticism from colleagues.
- Cost: A new buying decision means a new expenditure, even though it may be relatively small.

The salesman overcomes risk by supporting his case with good third-party references, on the argument that they can't all be fools, and by making the decision easy through skillful closing. He might also stress the guarantee aspects of his product.

He overcomes objections to inconvenience by showing that the long-term *value of the benefits* of the new product is worth any short-term inconveniences caused by the transition.

He overcomes satisfaction with present conditions by showing just how much better the new product will be, how much saving it will give, and how much happier everyone will be with it.

He overcomes fear of criticism from colleagues by stressing the increased value of the product and by ensuring that the customer has at hand all the counterarguments he needs.

He overcomes objections to new cost by showing that the new decision brings new real value for a relatively small increase in price.

Hesitancy in making a decision is natural and normal, and the possibility should therefore have been handled earlier in the sale (see Chapter 7). If it has been properly prehandled, the salesman need only refer back to the agreements reached at that time. The customer's restatement of the same objection is therefore handled by reminding him of the previous agreement and by reemphasizing the importance of the decision.

If the possibility of hesitancy has not been prehandled and the customer hesitates, the salesman must *close* decisively to increase pressure and to cut off the alternative avenues of escape. The commitment he now seeks also effectively checks the sincerity of the objections:

C. I won't need it for a few months yet.
S. When do you think you'll want it by?

C. November.

S. Good. Let's place the order immediately for delivery in November.

Or

C. I'd still like to think it over.

S. You said you'd buy the product if it did the things you wanted. You've agreed that it will do these things. What now is left to think over?

Or

C. I really should put the decision before my partners.

S. But earlier you said you were able to place the order alone.

C. Well, I've changed my mind now.

S. When you make the decision, presumably you'll want delivery as soon after as possible?

C. Yes.

S. This is normally the case. In order that we can plan delivery for you when you want it, may I suggest that we put the order in now, but subject to confirmation in writing on your partners' decision?

In this last example, the salesman increases pressure on the customer and then lets him settle for a provisional order. If his argument about his partners is sincere, there is no good reason why he should not place his order on this basis, and probably the salesman will receive confirmation within a week. If, on the other hand, his objection is insincere, he will refuse even the provisional order and the salesman must say:

"What really is the reason for your hesitation?"

The desire to avoid the decision can be seen as the customer raises a number of small doubts, each of which hardly requires an answer. Wait and listen to him without interruption until he indicates that he wants an answer. Answer him, close firmly, and remain silent.

The customer may also desire to avoid the decision because he is not really the decision maker. In this case, you should not have allowed the sale to proceed so far. If you have any doubts, it might be important to check again that he is the decision maker and that he can make this decision alone.

Or the customer may desire to avoid the decision because it precludes alternative choices. The customer wants to be doubly convinced. The way to do this is by summarizing:

- Resummarize your joint agreement on the criteria for ordering.
- Resummarize his commitment to make a decision, given during the trial close.
- Resummarize the enormous benefits of your product.
- Resummarize your joint agreement that the benefits of your product match his requirements.
- Now *close.*

Close firmly and remain silent. If he starts talking, continue to remain silent until you are absolutely forced to speak again. Then answer his question, close firmly again, and remain silent. Follow this pattern as long as necessary.

Prejudice in the customer's attitude should have been identified earlier and prehandled. At this point in the sale, perhaps the best step is to challenge his prejudice by asking him why he has set his mind in this way when the advantages he would gain from a decision are so overwhelming. But first, resummarize the agreements that were reached when you established the criteria for ordering, when you trial closed, and when you matched the benefits of your product to his requirements.

Usually the basis for prejudice is illogical, so logical argument is unlikely to prevail against it. An alternative is to rephrase your proposition in such a way that it will not conflict with his prejudice. Even though acceptance of the new proposal may assume acceptance of the original proposition, the customer is likely to be grateful that you have provided a means for him to make his decision.

Sheer cussedness should also have been identified and challenged earlier. At this point in the sale, the only step is to resummarize the agreements that have already been reached. Do this seriously and with the attitude that you are there to help, not to disagree. If this fails to make him aware of his ungraciousness, turn his objection back to him as a question, using the word *why,* and make him answer it himself. Then perhaps he will see that he is being unreasonable. And smile.

C. I prefer dirty vehicles to half-clean vehicles.
S. Why do you prefer dirty vehicles?

Although emotional objections can be harrassing at times, particularly when you know the weight of argument is on your side, it is vital not to be drawn into a sparring match with the customer. The first heavy blow you land will knock the order right out the door. Self-control at this time is indispensable.

If you feel yourself getting out of control, begin your reply with "I can understand why you said that," even if you can't. It is better than counting up to ten, and it starts your answer the right way.

Facetious objections are another way in which the customer can avoid the decision. Really he is doing no more than trying you out. If he can persuade you to rush out after his rabbit, he will see you as a fool, and this will give him the real reason he needs to decide not to do business with you.

The skill in overcoming facetious objections is in turning the objection back as a question. Because the objection was facetious in the first place, the customer is committed either to answer it or to deny it. Whichever he chooses, he will probably stop making facetious objections.

C. I like mud. It holds my trucks together.

S. But if you had the choice between buying an ordinary truck and one that never gets dirty, which would you choose?

C. The one that never gets dirty, of course.

S. So clean trucks are worth something to you?

Or

C. What makes you think the world would be a better place if trucks were cleaner?

S. Do you think the world would be a better place if trucks were dirtier?

Or

C. I like dirty trucks.

S. Why do you bother to paint your name on them, then?

Overcoming reasoned objections

Objections can come at any time in the sale, but it is not always wise to answer them right away. You can choose when to answer them:

- Immediately, if the objection does not disrupt your presentation or if your answer could enhance your proposal.
- Later, if it fits better into your presentation then or allows you to devote more time to it.

Similarly, you can choose the way to answer an objection:

- Directly, if it benefits your presentation.
- Indirectly, if the answer becomes self-evident through another part of your presentation.
- Not at all, if you feel the objection is worthless and it will only harden the customer's resistance if you try to answer it.

If you come back to an objection, restate it and ask the customer if he still requires a reply.

If the objection has nothing to do with the sale, acknowledge it and do not answer it.

Where the answer to one objection also answers other as yet unstated objections, provide the answer and show how it accounts for the other objections. In this way, you can sweep away areas of potential objection.

If an objection is based on a weak argument, you can handle it by reducing it to logical absurdity, without seeming to mock the customer; or you can compare the situation the customer is evoking with one that he more readily understands:

C. How can I know you'll repair the machine if it breaks down on a Saturday?
S. Well, a lot of our customers want their machines to work on Saturdays and, of course, they don't all break down on that day. However, we have to be in a position to repair them when they do. What do you do when one of your delivery trucks breaks down on a Saturday?

Basically, there are three ways to handle a reasoned objection:

- You can *outweigh* it by showing how far the advantages outweigh the disadvantages.
- You can *overcome* it by showing that it is not a problem at all.
- You can *weaken* it by showing that it is not such a serious problem in practice.

To sell the advantages of your product well, you have to be fully aware of the disadvantages. Only then can you show how the advantages outweigh the disadvantages.

Conversely, you can point out a minor disadvantage to lend weight to a corresponding major advantage. It makes you sound disarmingly frank. However, be careful not to encourage new fears by introducing the customer to problems he has not thought of before. These can only increase his sense of risk and doubt and, therefore, prejudice the sale. If you do manage to put a new fear into his mind, the chances are you will not be able to remove it.

If you feel that, in a particular case, the disadvantages outweigh the advantages, do not give up or even appear resigned. It is not *your* decision. Your job is to present your case the best way possible. The decision is up to the customer.

Once you know the disadvantages of your product, you must also know the solutions to them. You must have sufficient solutions to be able to handle the objections in any one of the many special situations where you will find them. The only way to find out how many solutions you have is to list the disadvantages and list the solutions beside them. Think of all the different categories of customers you have—and be sure not to lose that list!

As the disadvantages of your product will tend to be the same for each category of customer, so will their statements of their objections. You will learn to expect certain types of objection from certain categories of customer. However, the full meaning of the objection will vary according to the individual customer and his view of his own particular needs. It is therefore a good rule, whenever you hear an objection, to *check for understanding and for the reason behind the objection:*

> "Would I be right in saying that this is what is troubling you . . . ?
> Why does this trouble you especially?"

You have got to be able to see the target clearly if you are going to give yourself your best chance of hitting it.

If an objection cannot be outweighed or overcome, the strength of it can still be weakened. This can be done by stressing to the customer that the problem he sees so clearly in his mind is not so important in practice. The favorable experience of well-known existing customers can be mentioned as references to support your claim, and a quick telephone call to one of your contacts could well be sufficient to relieve his anxiety.

Alternatively, you could acknowledge that these are indeed problems, then give examples from your existing customers—how they have overcome the problem and, particularly, the enormous benefits they receive as a result of using your product. This is a good way to bring reality to your use of third-party references.

Remember that the customer thinks of you as the expert. He does not expect your product to be faultless, so do not claim it is. He does need to be able to place his confidence in you.

If the objections are of a minor operational nature, treat them as minor and handle them carefully but assumptively:

> "I really don't think you'll find this a problem when the machine is installed. If you do, I hope you'll call me and I'll see that the matter is handled for you."

If, at any stage in the sale, the customer voices an objection and you provide the answer, do not just leave it there. Before you go a step further, ask him if he is satisfied that you have answered his question for him. You have answered his question only when he agrees that you have answered it:

> "Are you happy that this answers your question?"

The meeting at which you hit the final objections is the meeting at which you should close the order. The customer's desire to buy is at its highest: he wants to make the decision and only awaits satisfaction to his final objection:

> "How am I going to get planning permission?"

Whatever you do, do not be pressured into leaving the room to run after solutions. By the time you arrive breathless back in his office, he will have grown cold on the whole thing; and he will probably have thought up two or three more problems for you to run away with and solve. Whenever you find yourself in the situation where the final objection cannot be handled across the desk, take the order on a provisional basis subject to a satisfactory solution to the problem.

Always be confident when handling objections. Be precise, be factual, and be sincerely interested. Your customer does not think his objections are a joke, and even if he appears flippant, you should treat his objections seriously. Do not overstate your case, or exaggerate. Be polite, and when he states his objection, acknowledge that his point is a good one and thank him for introducing it into the conversation:

> "That's a very good point, and I'm glad you mentioned it."

Somehow it must have escaped your attention!

To handle objections effectively, you must know exactly what your customer wants and what your product will do under every circumstance. There is always more than one way to view the same problem and your ability to understand the difference can determine whether you take the order. The customer must be made to see the product the way that you see it.

If you hesitate in answering an objection, the chances are that you will lose the customer's confidence.

Objections lead naturally into a closing sequence:

> C. I don't like red, but I'd take one if I could have a blue one.
> S. If I could give you a blue one, would you place your order? (*Trial close, testing to see whether the objection is sincere or insincere.*)
> C. Yes, I certainly would.
> S. Excellent. Let's fill this contract out now and specify a blue one.

Similarly:

> C. I'd buy one if it copied onto plain, ordinary paper.
> S. Why do you require copies on ordinary paper? (*To find out the hidden meaning behind the objection*)
> C. We send a lot of copies of our correspondence to our associates overseas and the special papers tend to be heavier.

The salesman now has an alternative, depending on the type of equipment he is selling:

Either:

> "Our equipment does copy onto ordinary paper. In fact you can copy onto both sides of one sheet, and that would make air-mailing very much cheaper. This is a sample of the paper we use. If you're satisfied that this is ordinary paper, are you happy to go ahead with your order?"

Or:

> S. Our equipment in fact copies onto special paper. However, if I could show you that it weighs less (costs no more to mail!) than the paper used in other equipment, would you be prepared to place your order with me? (*Shows examples of both*)
> C. Yes.
> S. Fine. Would you like delivery immediately, or would you prefer to wait until next week? (*Closing on the alternative close*)

Competition as an objection

The salesman must prehandle the possibility of competition while he establishes the customer's criteria for ordering. If he does the job properly, and if there is in fact another product under consideration, he should be able to draw out the competitor's name. Once he knows the competitor, he knows the best way to direct his own presentation.

The main battle against known competition takes place while the salesman established the customer's criteria for ordering (see Chapter 6). His success depends on his ability to establish new criteria that the competitor cannot satisfy.

This is not as difficult as it might seem. The customer has already met the competitor's salesman and has managed to avoid a decision; but his level of interest has been raised. Also, he is beginning to hear things that the other salesman did not tell him. (*These are the two dangers of leaving a customer without first taking his order!*)

If you can establish new criteria to suit his needs, the competitive alternative will fade to insignificance. If, on the other hand, the competition continues to present a real alternative, you can show how far the enormous advantages of your product *outweigh* the advantages of the competitive product, particularly in terms of value for the money. After all, why else would so many famous companies choose to use your products?

Throughout this time, the salesman must not use the competitor's name, even if the customer has given the name. It will only increase the customer's confidence in the competitor.

If the customer is resolute and will not modify his criteria for ordering, the sale is hardly worth continuing. Say something that will put a little fear into his heart, and go and call on another customer where the likelihood of a sale is greater:

> "Well, I'm sure you're making the best decision. But if you run into terrible problems when the product is installed, please don't forget to give me a call. Here is my card."

If the customer begins the negotiation by saying that he intends to buy a competitor's product, it gives the salesman a wonderful opportunity to establish his presentation through the trial close:

> C. Well, Mr. Lund, I don't think there's much point in our talking together. I have more or less decided to go ahead and order the Stoughton product. But tell me what you've got to offer anyway.
>
> S. Mr. Chadwick, that's a very, very good product and a good choice for you to make. But let me ask you, if my product can do better and less expensively all the things the competitive product can do, and also give you other advantages that I think will be important to you as well, would you be prepared to reconsider your decision seriously?

Of course the answer is yes. Now force him to say it:

> "Yes."

Sometimes, in selling, you think the competitive alternative has been prehandled. You successfully go through benefit selling, summarize, and close. And the customer remains unconvinced:

> C. No, Mr. Lund, I'm not really persuaded. I think I'm going to go ahead with the other product.
>
> S. Why do you say that?

In this instance, you cannot avoid mentioning competition directly by name. The choice is to sink or swim.

You must first reestablish the customer's criteria for ordering so that they match your product. Then list his criteria on a piece of paper and draw two columns, one for the competitor's product and one for your own. Now ask the customer which product best meets his requirements for each criteria. Obviously, your column is going to end up with more ticks—not necessarily all of them, but most of them. The customer now has visual proof that your product better matches his requirements. Ask him if he agrees with the conclusion, summarize, and close.

Throughout this process, praise your competitor's product. It is not that his is no good; it is just that yours is better.

If you fail in this attempt, at least you have tried. If you go away and still have a niggling feeling that your product is the one best suited for this company, perhaps the time has come to contact the top man.

Otherwise the rules for selling against competition are the same (see Chapter 8).

Never knock it—not even when it is breathing hard down your neck; and not even when it has been chosen in preference to your own products. You never know when you may be invited to go back.

Sell against your competitors' weaknesses. There are things you can do that they cannot do, benefits you have that they do not have. To do this well, you must know your competitors inside out. Their products may be more expensive in a certain way, their benefits may not be all they appear, they may have the problem of an awkward contract.

When you talk about your competitors, *emphasize the ones that are hopelessly out of the race.* Lavish praise on their professional approach. Compliment what they do not do well, or what they do well that does not matter very much.

Use the overwhelming weaknesses of competitive products to spotlight your own benefits by comparison, though, again, do not mention the competitors by name. Do not say anything about them that is even vaguely untrue. Otherwise you too will meet your Watergate.

Remember too that, all other things being equal, the difference between two products is the difference between the two people selling them. If you are faced with a customer who is leaning toward a competitor, treat it as an insult to your own ability and give yourself a kick up the backside for not getting there sooner.

Price as an objection

Once you have finished benefit selling, summarize for agreement and *close*. Then the customer, unless he has become totally infatuated by the dulcet tones of your golden voice, is going to say to you:

> "Tell me, first, how much is it all going to cost?"

You have met the price objection and it must be carefully handled.

Price can only be an objection. It can never be a selling benefit. No one wants to spend money if he doesn't have to. No one buys anything because it is cheap. He must want it first. So cost can never be the reason for buying. Even when a product brings a saving in current expenditure, it means payment in a different way. It means a new contract or a new amortization over a new period of time. It means another decision.

Price must therefore always be described in its most glamorous form. If cost per unit looks best, then presentation of cost must be on a per unit basis. It is often easier to sell 5¢ a unit than it is to sell $2,500, even though the customer will get 50,000 units for that expenditure. If you can show the unit cost is reasonable, you have at least some chance of agreeing on total cost.

Similarly, daily or weekly total costs look better than annual or capital costs. Remember, 25¢ a day isn't much, but 25¢ every day for a year is $91.25.

Make sure you know the arguments that support your figures, though. If the customer is able to show that you are underestimating cost, he will assume your purpose is malicious, and you will lose his confidence.

Show price as a daily or weekly cost and relate it to a cost that is familiar in the customer's everyday life:

> "That is less than the cost of a gallon of gas."

Use a pencil and paper to show price in its simplest terms. Particularly if your customer has to go to his Board, make sure he understands how the total price is constructed.

Show price as value. For additional price, show additional value. Relate your price to your customer's current expenditure to show better value.

If your product is more expensive than a competitor's, you will have to show additional value (*benefits*) to cover the additional price. The customer does not buy the cheapest. He buys what he thinks is the best value for the money.

A product that is highly priced can seem less expensive when compared with a product of an even higher price.

In selling products for processing in manufacturing, the importance of price depends on its influence on final costs. If the percentage is small, the buyer will often prefer to pay rather more in order to get, for example, better throughput on his machines or better deliveries. Expensive production holdups will quickly absorb small savings in the purchase price of the raw material. To sell higher price in these instances, therefore, requires the salesman to sell the benefits of better throughput and better deliveries.

Generally, lower prices increase margins. However, in retail outlets where margins are often fixed as a percentage of purchase price, lower purchase prices could lead to a fall in revenue, and therefore a lower profit per unit of sales. In this case, the salesman would have to show lower prices in terms of larger sales and higher total revenue.

Don't become overconscious of the price level yourself. If you make out the best case for the product, the customer will decide whether it is expensive or not. Anyway, the customer is already experiencing a comparable cost in his present system or a comparable loss in not having what he should have, both of which can be shown.

If you can accept that $100 means less to a rich man than to a poor man, you should be able to accept that $1,000 has a different value for a company and for an individual. In business, it is a company's money that is being spent and not an individual's. Moreover, whereas individuals tend to look at expenditure as cost, companies look at it as investment for profit.

The more expensive your product is, the closer you must stay to your sales presentation. It is too easy to allow the customer additional leeway because, in your heart, you know the decision is big for him. In effect, it is a lack of confidence on your part and this lack of confidence will be transmitted.

One thing you can be sure of: if you think your product is expensive, your customer is bound to think the same way. If you really do think it is expensive, you had better make up your mind on the ways it gives full value for the money before you make your first call. If you cannot do this, you will not succeed in selling—and you probably should not even try.

Don't let yourself be drawn into bargaining over price. Your product is either worth what you are asking or it is not. If you break the price, you lose credibility and put all your other sales claims in doubt. Your action is also likely to start a rumor among your other customers. If you must *take something off*, do it indirectly in payment terms or in trade-in values. Ideally, you should offer the same terms to all your customers.

Having established with your customer that your product gives value for the money, don't start adding on additional costs for items without which the original product would be worthless or unsuitable. It destroys any feeling of value for the money and it can only irritate your customer.

Similarly, don't start introducing the idea of minimum orders or minimum product packages at this stage in the sale. That should be introduced as part of the total program at the time the salesman introduces his proposal to the customer (see the section "The Salesman's Statement of Intent" in Chapter 5). At that time, objections to the nature of the sales proposal can be properly prehandled. Otherwise, the customer will think you are taking him for a ride and will resent the way you do business with him.

Don't threaten your customers with price increases. On the other hand, if you are coming up for a price increase, you should make your customers aware of it and give them the chance to place their orders beforehand.

The more important your product is to the customer, the less important its price is to him and the more he will pay for it. The more important the salesman is able to make his product seem, the less likely the customer is to find price as an objection.

If, with all costs considered, you can show the customer that your total weekly cost is lower than his current weekly cost, it would be cheaper for him to throw his existing equipment away, even if it is still relatively new. However, this may be a difficult decision for him to make politically and it is probably the political objection that you will have to overcome. You might try an appeal to his pride. Alternatively, you could find him a buyer for his existing plant.

If the customer shows you that your product costs more than a competitor's, stress how much more value it will give him. After all, does he think that if your competitor was offering *better value*, you would be working for your present company? Besides, when it comes to actually getting the stuff there on time, your deliveries are second to none:

> "Phone Mr. Longman of Resnick and Company. He used to use an alternative supplier."

When the customer says that your product is too expensive, don't just disagree and become involved in an argument you can only lose. Ask him *why* he thinks it is too expensive. Then when you have his reasoning, you have some chance of handling his objection.

Sometimes the sale will collapse during price discussions, and the simple reason is that the customer does not want to buy. Be aware of this possibility. If this is in fact the case, the sale should never have reached this stage. You should have been able to isolate the main objection earlier:

> "What is really troubling you?"

Discussion of price should be started only after you have had the opportunity to summarize and agree on the benefits of your product. This, of course, is logically necessary before you can show value. If the customer brings up questions on price earlier in the sale, you must succeed in delaying your full answer. Otherwise he will see all cost and no value:

C. How much does it cost?

S. I'll obviously be coming to price later. If I may, I'd like to talk about it when I have a clearer idea of what you want.

C. But approximately what does it cost? What is the price range?

S. It works out to about 85¢ a week. That's less than it costs you to wash your car. You said. . . .

C. But what is the full capital cost?

S. Surely, the first thing for us to do is to decide whether you want it. Then we can discuss price and you can decide whether it is value for the money. As I was saying. . . .

Obviously, the salesman need go only as far as the customer's questions. This situation is one of the few exceptions in the sales presentation where the salesman uses statements rather than questions. Questions now would only invite the answer you did not want. In this situation, therefore, make a statement answer to each of the customer's questions and immediately try to go on with your presentation.

Price is the last objection. Your task is to show that the price is reasonable for the benefits your product offers.

12 Summarizing Prior to Closing

Before going on to Stage 3 and *closing the sale*, it is essential that the salesman summarize to confirm the agreements he has reached with the customer on the match between his product benefits and the customer's requirements (see the section "Relating Benefits to Customer Criteria" in Chapter 10):

> "If I may now summarize: you said you wanted in the new product.... You've agreed that my product gives you these things because of its features.... Are you now happy that my product can satisfy your requirements?"

Similarly, it is vital that the salesman confirm with the customer that he has successfully answered his sincere objections (see the section "Overcoming Reasoned Objections" in Chapter 11):

> "Are you happy that this provides the answer to your question?"

Confirming these agreements is essential to ensure that:

- Nothing has been omitted.
- There are no outstanding misunderstandings.
- There is nothing left to do but *close* the sale.

13 Closing the Sale

The second call

It is not every customer that you can get to close the sale across the table at the first meeting—though you should try if you are going to take the order by the shortest route. Sometimes you have to go back for a second call.

The first rule for the second call is: *Always set the appointment for it before you leave the previous call.* It is very much easier to do than trying by telephone at a later date. Making extra telephone calls takes valuable time and costs money; and it gives the customer another opportunity to stall you. Once he learns to stall you, he will get bored with you.

The second rule is: *Call back only when you have something new to ask or to offer.* This is as true for a face-to-face call as it is for a telephone call. If you have nothing new to ask or offer, you should not call.

Particularly, do not keep on calling back for the order. You will only become a nuisance. Instead, work to a plan. If you have exhausted one plan, create another. At least this way you will bring a little interest into the customer's life.

Never get yourself into a situation where you are asking the customer whether he has changed his mind yet. If you do, you have not begun to sell. Selling has more to do with solving his problems than with promoting your products.

If you have made a market for your product with the customer, make sure you follow it up quickly. You are doing yourself a disservice if you let him hang fire. You could lose the order. You have set him up for the decision and there is a good chance your competitor will come along to take it.

It is unlikely that you will have to visit the customer more than four or five times for the initial order, whatever the product. If you take longer than this, there is probably something wrong with your technique and you will begin to lose orders because people will think you are bothering them.

Call in person on the customer's premises only when you have some physical reason for being there—something to show him, a site to check, a problem to handle, a quotation to deliver, a contract to sign. And do not let the customer persuade you to call unless there is good reason. If you have any doubts, ask him why he wants you to call. Do not let him waste your time if he has nothing better to do with his own.

A cold call in passing can be a good idea if you are looking for a final decision. If the customer has promised to have a decision for you, he cannot blame you for asking for it. A sudden, unexpected call can break his lethargy and precipitate the decision. He might have said, for example, that he wants to confirm it with his partner, and this he can do while you wait.

The second call, after a demonstration, should produce the order. You must insist that he keep to a timetable for his decision. If you have covered the ground, what else is there to tell him? Your conversation should now be one of conclusions: a resummary of the problem, a resummary of the product benefits and how they match his requirements, and perhaps a resummary of the evidence of a demonstration or a third-party reference. What is his final objection? Remind him of the commitments he has undertaken, and *close*.

A site call fits in well as a second call. You might, however, have begun your presentation initially with a walk to see where the product *will* be used.

Site calls are useful to stress operational user benefits. Talk in word pictures. Make believe that the machine is already installed, and that the employees are enjoying using it with twice their normal productivity.

In equipment selling, do not make a big fuss over problems of delivery and installation. Be a professional. You should know almost by eye whether delivery is possible. Take the basic measurements and state the basic site requirements. Do not start lifting floorboards to show how clever you are. Your job is to sell. If the installation specialists find the equipment will not go in, the order will have to be canceled. It is better to cancel an order you have than to lose one by fooling around.

Similarly, do not give professional advice on subjects you are not professionally equipped to handle. You will only make yourself liable for any damage that occurs, and upset the customer as well. If there is any doubt at all, take the order on a provisional basis, subject to the site requirements being suitable. Give it to him in writing if necessary, even if it means going next door and using his secretary's typewriter. But make sure you get that signature. You might not get another chance.

One word of warning: it seems that the more engineers and specialists you call in to "help" you before the order is taken, the less likelihood you have of taking the order. Generally, these specialists are not trained in persuasion, and even when they are, they are usually inept at it. There is an excellent chance that they will suggest new problems when they think they are solving others. Time passes; objectives become muddled both for you and for your customer. Suddenly he thinks that it is all becoming just too much trouble.

Keep the sale simple. Find the way to complete the negotiation without bringing in third parties. Avoid stressing problems. You do not want them, and the customer is certainly listening to you because he thinks you are going to take his problems away.

If during the second call you are invited to discuss the decision with other members of the company, make sure you go there fully prepared. For example, you will need new visual aids that the group can view together. If you fear dissenters among the new audience, take along a colleague who can separate them from the main group. But remember, only one of you should be doing the selling.

If you take a specialist with you, make sure he understands that he is to speak only when you ask him—and then in single sentences no longer than five words.

If you sit down with a new group, don't fall into the trap of assuming you have the same level of communication with them as you have with your original contact. Start the whole sale again from the beginning and deal with each step rigorously.

The technique is to use a précis of the agreements you have already established, showing how each was reached and the criteria that were considered. Bring your original contact into the conversation to confirm these agreements. Don't take the risk of omitting any part, even though it was fully covered in the previous conversation. An objection arising from such an omission can lead to new chains of objections which the group may not allow you to handle.

If you are selling to a group, select the man you think is the decision maker and make your presentation to him. Don't be diverted from this, except where politeness requires. Handle outside questions only if they are pertinent to the moment. Otherwise, ask the questioner if you may come back to that point later. Once you start letting in questions at random, they will multiply as one question sparks off another. Soon you will lose control and endanger the sale.

Once you reach the end of your presentation, ask the *decision maker* if he has any more questions—and then ask for the decision.

A basic rule in selling is: *Take the order just as soon as you can.* The first call is the best time, because the customer is most interested in your product. From then on, as the number of calls increases, the chances of taking the order diminish. If you missed the order the first time around, success on the second call is at a premium. You know the customer. You are in a position to design your presentation specifically for him. Smile, be friendly, be hard, be to the point. And *close.*

Knowing when to close

If a salesman cannot close, he cannot sell, however many words he uses. If you can do nothing else except ask for the order, you are part of the way toward becoming a salesman and a long way further than the man who has achieved a good presentation but cannot ask for the order.

The best chance to close is during the first call. At that time, the customer's interest is highest. At each subsequent call, the chance of success diminishes.

The first opportunity to close is the moment the customer indicates that he is ready to purchase. At that time, you stop whatever you are saying, wherever you are in your presentation, and ask him if he would like to place his order.

The customer usually indicates that he is considering the purchase by asking questions you would normally expect toward the end of the negotiation—questions on delivery times, trade-in values, maintenance, purchase provisions, contract details, decision times, trial order possibilities.

Conversely, the salesman can preempt these questions by bringing them into the negotiation himself:

    C. Is there any choice in the method of purchase?

    S. You can buy it either outright or through a lease contract. Which would you prefer? (*Direct close*)

Or

    S. When would you want installation by?

    C. November.

    S. If I could see that installation is made by November, would you be able to place your order now? (*Trial close*)

If there is specific information that the customer requires now in order to make his decision, he will ask the specific questions. The salesman will answer each of these questions in turn until the customer has the information he needs. Then he will say:

    S. Have I now answered all your questions satisfactorily? (*Choosing a direct question expecting the answer yes*)

    C. Yes.

    S. Fine. Shall we now go ahead and place your order?

    C. Yes.

The only danger in the customer's asking this kind of *final* question so early in the sale is that he might persuade the salesman to talk about price before he has finished explaining all the benefits that meet the customer's criteria. As the salesman is always selling value, he is well advised to make sure he covers all the customer's criteria before he moves to price, even if it means covering them more quickly. Otherwise, he is likely to create indecision by opening himself to questions on the product *after* he has given pricing information.

If the customer does not react to the salesman's close, the salesman can continue with his presentation where he left it, closing again each time the customer gives a *buying signal*. In this way, the salesman cannot close too often. In fact, he is more likely to lose the order by not closing often enough.

The second opportunity to close the sale comes when the customer asks enthusiastically about the product in such a way as to invite a trial close reply:

    C. Will it *really* wash any shape or size of vehicle clean in three minutes?

    S. Well, if I can show you that it will wash any one of your vehicles clean in three minutes, will you place an order for it?

Once again, the customer is left to ask questions for the specific information he requires prior to his decision; and if he chooses not to take up the challenge of the *trial close*, the salesman can again continue with his presentation as before.

The third opportunity to close the sale is the more formal situation where the close is the only logical step left in the negotiation. The salesman has established and summarized the criteria for ordering, the customer has agreed to make a decision based on satisfaction of these criteria, the salesman has proved that the benefits of the product are capable of meeting the customer's requirements, and he has handled the outstanding objections. Now, all he has left to say is:

"Are you now happy to go ahead with your order?"

If the sale has been judged properly, there is little chance the final close will fail.

Finally, the fourth opportunity to close the sale comes in the salesman's opening statement:

"My name is Lund. I work for the Wash-Clean Truck Washing Machine Company. We can wash any one of your vehicles, all over, in less than three minutes. Would you like one?" (*Direct close*)

If just may happen that the customer has already made up his mind to buy your product and has just been waiting for you to walk into his office. So why not give him the chance?

The salesman almost cannot get a bad reply to a close in the opening sentence. If the customer says yes, the order is taken right away. If he says no, the salesman asks: "Why not?" The sale is already in progress with the salesman establishing the customer's criteria for ordering. A customer's "Tell me more about it" invites the salesman to make his presentation.

Early in the sale, the salesman decides the path he is going to take to achieve his primary objective: the order. This he then breaks down into secondary objectives:

— Get him to agree to an appointment.
— Get him to accept suitable criteria for ordering.

— Get him to agree to a demonstration.
— Get him to agree that the product meets his needs.
— Get him to agree to place his order by the end of the week.

These are five interrelated objectives that must be closed before the order can be taken. All the way through this series, therefore, the salesman will be closing on each objective with such questions as:

"May I come to your office to talk about it?"

"Are you happy that these are in fact the criteria you wish to satisfy?"

"Would 10:00 on Wednesday be convenient for the demonstration, or would 3:30 on Thursday be more suitable?"

"Are you now happy that the product does in fact meet your needs?"

"Are you now happy to go ahead with your order?"

While you're learning to balance your presentation, adopt a plan that ends with the close. Keep to the close even when you have that irksome feeling that you are miles away from the order. It is the only way to learn, and you may be lucky. Many times, the abruptness of the request for the order precipitates the decision or, at least, the real objections.

Similarly, if you are unsure of where you are in the sale, close. It is a fine way to isolate the customer's response.

When you are selling a product well, you have the feeling at the point of the final close that you are not asking for the order but the customer is asking to place it.

At any time when the orders start pouring in, make sure you capitalize on your success. Telephone everyone you can think of who might be interested in placing his order as well:

"I'm in such a good mood. I've just sold to four companies in your industrial park and I had the feeling that, if I just telephoned you, you might be ready to order too. Would you like to order now?"

It sounds friendly and enthusiastic, it passes news of new customers, and it suggests that everyone else is making the decision, so why doesn't he?

Never be afraid to ask for a decision, even when you think the answer will be no. It might be yes and you cannot lose what you have not got.

In selling, always try to think to yourself: *I'm bound to be successful; it's just a question of when.* Don't give up. Keep going until you find the argument that will sell your product.

The ABC of selling is: *Always Be Closing.*

Knowing how to close

The first rule in knowing how to close is to ask for the order and then to be *silent.* Silence puts pressure on the customer. Pressure is necessary if you are to overcome the customer's natural reluctance to make a decision. Decisions are difficult for anyone, and the customer will resist.

If you start talking, you will release this vital pressure; and you will only end up answering your own questions.

If the customer sits there in silence and looks at you, just sit there in silence and look right back at him. He is as uncomfortable as you are, and you will win if you can stick it out.

If the customer starts talking, say nothing. Answer his questions only when he stops and insists on an answer. If he stops and says nothing, close him again with the same question.

You will never talk a customer into a buying decision by talking him to a point of exhaustion. It is easier to talk yourself out of a favorable decision than to talk yourself into it.

In the questions leading up to the final question, use questions expecting the answer ves. They will get the customer into the right mood:

S. You accept that, don't you?
C. Yes.

Unfortunately, it is too easy to use questions expecting the answer no, particularly when you feel the sale is going against you:

S. You don't accept that, do you?
C. No.

The questions expecting the answer no are weak questions, and the questions of the weak salesman. Ultimately they lead to:

S. Nothing today, then?
C. No, thank you.

There is no better time to be strong than when you come under pressure.

Be strong when you close. Be confident. Show no trace of uncertainty or nervousness. If you are uncertain or nervous, how is the customer meant to feel? It is his money.

Choose your words carefully. Do not use the kind of words that are likely to scare him. For example, it might be wise to use the word *we* rather than *you,* and *installation* rather than *order:*

"Shall *we* go ahead with the *installation,* then?"

It obviously reduces tension by putting you at the side of the customer as a joint decision maker. The "let's do this one together" approach can expedite the order, particularly where there are problems with Boards, site requirements, and so on.

Closing has to do with making the decision easy for the customer. Five out of the six closing techniques discussed in the next section deliberately avoid asking a direct question and assume that the decision has been made and that an agreement is really required only on matters of detail, such as the delivery dates.

Stressing product guarantees is another way to make the decision easier. Most companies should offer them in their contract. Guarantees build the customer's confidence in his decision.

Offering products on trial and taking the order on a provisional basis are two more ways for the salesman to make the customer's decision easier. However, it is bad policy to weaken your proposal any more than you need to. If you can take the order fully and properly in the first place, you should. You should offer trial periods and provisional orders only when this is the last resort open to you. Offering *free* trials or altering the usual contract terms to suit a particular customer should be countenanced only in very exceptional circumstances.

Mentioning when prices are about to be increased is a way to precipitate an order, though you must be careful not to appear to threaten the customer. Properly done, it is nice of you to give him the advance warn-ing. A coming price increase should always be made to yield a rash of orders, and some of them can initially be taken on a provisional basis:

> "Prices are going up next Monday and I thought I'd give you a call in case you were ready to place your order. If you're worried about getting the decision through your Board in time, we could take the order on a provisional basis subject to Board approval."

If the market is too large to be handled any other way, a price increase can effectively form the basis of a mailshot.

Similarly, if you are fortunate enough to be working for a company whose product is in high demand, the rapidly expanding delivery sched-ule can also be used to hasten orders.

Offering minimum *trial* quantities which are to be paid for is often the best method for the commodity salesman to break the grip of a single competitive supplier. Once you get the first order through—and make sure you deliver excellent quality—it is just a matter of getting the size of the orders to grow.

One way back to a customer who has said he would take a trial quantity is to say:

> "It just so happens that one of our trucks is coming your way to make a delivery to your next-door neighbor. Why don't I put that trial quantity on the truck for you?"

If you are selling *interdependent* products, do not try to close them one by one. It insults the customer's intelligence and his pocket. Put everything he needs together in a package and sell that. There is more chance of success, there is more profit in it, and he can always negotiate out what he does not need.

If you are selling several *independent* products, close one and get the signature before you close the second, and so on.

However, if you are selling a long line of products, for example to a retailer, don't ask for the decisions product by product. You will exhaust the customer before you have realized his full buying potential. Again, put all the goods together as a package and sell that. Then the customer can negotiate out what he does not require.

Once the customer starts signing, he will sign more than once. If you are selling equipment and, depending on the success of the first installation, the customer will order two more, close the other two contracts on a provisional basis. You will find this much easier, and it will take much less time, than calling back month after month and asking him if he is now happy enough to proceed with the new installations.

If you want to obtain a decision in an area where you know there is an illogical, emotional objection, rather than closing against this objection rephrase your proposal into one that is acceptable to the customer, even though acceptance of the new proposal assumes acceptance of the original proposal. It lets the customer off his own hook and he will be grateful for it.

Similarly, if you are telephoning for a final decision on your proposal and you think the answer will be no, do not wait for disaster. Once he learns to say no to you, he will tend to turn down any future proposal you make. So adjust your proposal, even if only slightly, to allow for a new negotiation. If his answer was yes, he will insist on it anyway. If it was no, you will not lose him. However, be careful not to offer an alternative program that is vastly different from the one you were offering, or you will lose his confidence.

If the product you are selling does not have to meet an exact specification and you are trying to decide whether to sell high or low, sell high. *More* normally costs more and the customer's natural reluctance to spend money will temper his purchase decision. Selling too low is really a bigger problem than selling too high, particularly when the product fails to meet requirements the next year.

If you feel in your heart that the customer should not be buying at all, the honest thing to do is not to sell. It is usually the wisest thing to do. Bad selling leads to dissatisfied customers who are bad references for your product.

If the decision is not reached at this interview, do not lose the initiative. Make sure, before you leave, that you establish what remains to be done before the order can be taken, a timetable for further action, and a date and time for the next meeting. If you cannot get this, go for the next best thing, which is a date and time you can telephone him.

If the customer says no, there is no reason to give up there and then. Ask him *why* he says no, and check to see if his reasons have any validity. If they don't, present the countervailing evidence. There is more than one way to look at a problem. If you think his objections have validity, but that the evidence in favor of your proposal is stronger, present this evidence to outweigh his objections.

Remember, for every disadvantage there is an advantage. It is just that some of these advantages are a little more difficult to find.

It is a point, however, that the more you let the sale slide into argument, the less chance you have of making the sale. In fact, if you have handled the sale properly, you should not get the no at the stage of the close. The objection should have come out earlier in the sale, when you were better able to handle it.

With a no at this stage, it is important to avoid conflict, and questions again become important:

"*Why* do you say that?"

Or

"If we look at that problem another way, do you think this could provide the solution?"

If you lose the decision, be tactful, Do not lose your temper, become rude, tell him he doesn't know what he is doing, become insulted. He might become your customer again at a later date. He might join another company, or his present company might vary its methods to include your products. Anyway, there is little satisfaction in blasting off at people you hardly know. It just isn't worth the emotional effort.

On the other hand, if you feel you are being shut out of the decision, because of either malice or bribery, you can decide to go over his head to the president. The man you are negotiating with is, first and foremost, an employee of his company. If he fails to act to the benefit of his company for personal reasons, he must be able to defend his position and, ultimately, to take any consequences.

It must be stressed, however, that before you can claim an unfair decision your proposal must be able to demonstrate substantial advantages over the alternative methods. There are no prizes for becoming involved in personal vendettas. They are harmful both to you and to your company. For this reason, even if you suspect malice or bribery, you must never suggest it. Leave it to the president to find out for himself. Like Caesar's wife, you must be beyond reproach.

Overpersistence, or foot-in-the-door selling, comes from overstressing the features of your product and failing to persuade the customer that it provides a solution to his problem. It also comes from weak closing. It is better to close the order forcefully at the right time than to weaken this close and then have to go on nagging for a decision afterward. At the right time, the customer will feel like making a decision, however difficult he may find it. If that moment is lost, the salesman's repeated recalls only remind the customer of his problem, and not of its solution.

Whatever you do, do not beg for business. If you cannot take orders on ability, you should not be selling.

Six closing techniques

If the salesman does not actually ask for the order, the chances are he will never get it.

A good salesman is able to decide which close he will use as he begins his presentation. He will then adapt the form of his presentation to achieve that close.

There are many different ways to close a sale, and some clearly suit certain products better than others. Some, however, also suit certain types of customer better, so the salesman should be sufficiently practiced in his closing skills to be able to handle any situation he is likely to find.

The many different ways to close a sale are the many different words and sentences the salesman can use in closing. Basically, however, they all evolve from the following techniques:

> The direct close
> The assumptive close
> The alternative close
> The step-by-step close
> The supposition close
> The provisional order close

The direct close

The direct close is the direct question asking the customer whether he would like to place his order:

> "Are you happy to place your order now?"

Or

> "Shall we go ahead and arrange installation?"

It could also be a series of closing questions which follow each other
logically:

S. Would you like one?
C. Yes, I think so.
S. Good. What is the full name and address of your company?
   (*Filling out the order form*)

The direct close has the advantage of being direct, abrupt, and to the
point. It leaves the customer very little room for maneuver and is therefore a *strong* close. It puts the question to him directly without any
softening. His answer can be either yes or no.

A customer's no would be followed by the salesman's technique for
handling objections:

"Why not?"

The direct close is ideal when the customer indicates a strong desire
to buy and offers no major objections.

It is also used to put pressure on a customer who is finding minor
objections in order to avoid the decision. Here the salesman would
handle the minor objection and direct close after it in order to put
pressure on the customer to avoid seeking other minor objections:

"Are you *now* happy to make your decision?" (That is, *When
are you going to make up your mind?*)

The assumptive close

The assumptive technique is used throughout the sale (see the section
"Assumptive Selling" in Chapter 6):

"*When* you have the product, you will find. . . . "

When, rather than *if*, paints the picture of the decision having already
been made. The salesman *assumes* throughout his presentation that the
customer will buy.

The *assumptive close* now assumes that the decision to buy is yes
and that it is just a matter of getting the details:

"*How* would you like to pay for it?"

"*When* would you like delivery?"

"*Where* would you like it placed?"

Using the assumptive close is a matter of phrasing questions, usually beginning HOW, WHEN, or WHERE. As the salesman asks these assumptive questions one after the other, and the customer answers, the customer begins to imagine that he has already made the decision. The decision itself, however, is never made directly, and the explicit question requesting the decision is never asked:

S. When would you like delivery?
C. I'd like it in November.
S. Fine. If you just sign here I'll see that delivery is made in November and that installation is carried out to your require-ments on this site.

As the assumptive close avoids the request for a decision to buy, the salesman uses it in those cases where he thinks the customer is nervous about making a decision and will react badly to a direct close question.

The assumptive close can also be used in selling quantities:

"Shall we place the order for the five?"

However, because it suggests the alternative "five or none," it should generally be used in commodity selling only where the salesman is building up a total order of different items. For other salesmen, the alternative close is a better way to sell quantities.

Asking the customer if he would like "any" or "anything else" is a hopeless way to close for a salesman. It is totally negative and suggests the answer "none" or "nothing today, thank you." In this situation you must always specify a number or the specific second product:

"Would you like a nice new tie to go with that shirt?"

The alternative close

The alternative close is again an assumptive close, but offers the cus-tomer the choice of an alternative. It assumes that the decision has been made but that it is just a matter of choice and quantities, delivery times, payment schemes, sizes, patterns, colors: in fact, anything where choice can be offered:

> "Would you like a big red one or a big blue one?"

> "Would you like to rent it, or buy it on an installment plan?"

> "Would you like it delivered next week or would you prefer to wait a week?"

The customer would reply "neither" only if he thought that the salesman was trying to force him into a decision too early, in which case the salesman would continue with his presentation where he left it.

The choice of size or quantities in the alternative close will positively influence the size or value of the orders taken. So choose the figures carefully.

The alternative close has the customer deciding between the alternatives rather than whether he wants one at all. A decision between alternatives must mean an order of some kind. A good salesman may decide to offer the right customer two units, knowing that at least he will place the order for one.

The alternative close is ideal when the salesman is a little unsure of the exact specifications of the customer's requirement. The choice he offers can then be the range of alternatives. He would target in on one so he could sell that strongly, but protect his position with the alternative.

On the other hand, it can be worthwhile to offer a choice even when the alternative is not one the customer would choose. This will leave the situation open for the customer to make his own decision for the obvious choice:

> "No, no, I think I would prefer this one."

The alternative close is particularly important in closing for an appointment on the telephone: you offer the customer an alternative of times to avoid discussion on whether he should even see you or not.

Otherwise, as a final close, the alternative close should be used in situations where the assumptive close would also be appropriate.

The step-by-step close

The step-by-step close is a technique in which the salesman directs the main decision by asking for a number of small related decisions that the customer has no difficulty in accepting. However, by accepting the small decisions, the customer ultimately feels himself committed to the main decision. In effect, the salesman has reduced the terror of the main decision by allowing the customer to make his decision in parts.

This closing technique is normally used in three situations. The first is when the salesman has a detailed order form to complete. Instead of asking directly for the decision, he assumes acceptance, pulls out his order form, and starts completing it. His questions are for information he needs for the form. On completion, he passes the form and pen over to the customer and says:

"Will you sign here, please?"

It is essential throughout this close that the salesman maintain his confidence. One moment of doubt will cause the customer to feel that he is not doing *the most normal thing.*

The second situation in which this close is used is where the purchase decision requires the customer to decide on several small matters of detail. Buying a car is an example of this. The salesman again assumes acceptance of the purchase and offers the customer instead the choice of specifications:

S. Have you decided between red and blue?
C. Yes, I want the red.
S. Do you want wire wheels or chromed rims?
C. Wire wheels, I think.
S. What color upholstery, beige or cinnamon?
C. Cinnamon.
S. Fine. Let's start getting some of the details down on paper. (*That is, the order form*)

The third situation in which the step-by-step close is used is where the salesman has established a number of agreements in his negotiation with the customer. He now resummarizes these agreements with the objective of obtaining a number of yeses from the customer prior to the final yes:

> S. Are you happy that the equipment will give you the vehicle cleanliness you want?
> C. Yes.
> S. Are you happy that it will fit comfortably into your existing garage?
> C. Yes.
> S. Are you happy with price?
> C. Yes.
> S. Fine. Let's go ahead with the installation, then.
> C. Yes.

This yes technique is also used where the salesman has hit an unexpected no in another close and feels the need to resummarize for yeses prior to closing again.

The supposition close

The supposition close is a conditional close and related to the trial close (see the section "The Trial Close to Establish Commitment" in Chapter 6).

The trial close is used throughout the sale to establish commitment and to handle objections:

> "*If I* can satisfy you that we can handle this problem, *will you* place your order with us?"

It is used as a final close only when the salesman says:

> "You said that if I could satisfy you that we can handle this problem, you would place your order with us. You have agreed that we can handle the problem. Will you now place your order with us?"

The supposition close uses the same conditional sentence in a slightly simpler form:

> "If it were blue, would you buy one?"

You would ask the question if you had a blue one to offer, or if you felt his request for a blue one was insincere.

This technique can work when the customer is showing a minor hang-up and feels he cannot say yes to your original proposal. He is looking for an honorable settlement, and you should give it to him.

It is also useful as an answer to the customer who says he would buy one if it was blue. But rather than jump in, order form in hand, to confirm that you have a blue one, ask him:

> "Why do you want a blue one?"

You must understand the reason for his question if you are to give him the answer he needs before he will sign (see Chapter 11).

The provisional order close

The provisional order close should really be used only when circumstances beyond your control would otherwise delay the signing of the full order—for example, requirements for Board or budgetary approval, for site survey, or for planning permission. It enables you to achieve your primary objective, which is to take the order now:

> "If I may suggest this, why don't you place your order now on a provisional basis, to be confirmed in writing on Board approval? From our point of view it will help us in planning your delivery and requisitioning your equipment. From your point of view it will mean you can have your installation just as soon as we receive your Board's approval."

The provisional order close has the advantage of taking the order at a time when the customer thinks he is delaying his decision. The sales argument is reasonable and logical. If the customer has been sincere in his negotiation, it is difficult for him to say no to this proposal. He feels he can sign the order without responsibility; but, by doing so, he passes over any emotional resistance he might have to the decision. He will then inevitably confirm his order because, in his mind, he has made the decision, although he felt no risk when he did so.

The provisional order close bypasses problems, such as planning requirements, over which you have no control. It makes the customer more active in their solution because, having made the decision, he wants the product. It also means you do not have to prejudice your sale with too many follow-up calls asking, "Have you got planning permission yet?"

The provisional order close can be used to avoid demonstrations and boardroom decisions completely:

> "Why don't you place a provisional order with me now, which must be confirmed in writing before delivery can take place? It will place your name on our delivery schedule. If you still want the product after the demonstration (or after you have discussed it with your colleagues), confirm the order with me in writing. Otherwise, I'll cancel it by the end of the month."

Again, this proposal is difficult for the customer to refuse reasonably; and you have achieved three important objectives: you have taken his signature, you have his decision in your favor, and you have set a final deadline for the order. The chances are the customer, having made his decision, will telephone within the week to ask you to forget the demonstration and to make your delivery as soon as possible.

Your contract or order form should be designed to allow you to take orders this way, and you should carry the right letters of guarantee to place in the customer's hand.

When the customer is first convinced he should have your product, he is most likely to sign. Once you walk out the door without his signature, a wall of problems will rise behind you. You've let him off the hook and let him go. You've broken his sense of commitment to the negotiation. Getting back can be a real problem. So you must do everything in your power to leave with a signed order of some kind in your pocket; and a provisional order goes a long way toward satisfying this requirement.

Handling the contract

There is no marketing value in conditions of sale that can be unraveled only by a lawyer. Clever legal jargon and oblique references to little-known laws can only create doubt and prejudice sales. It is unlikely that a company will take its customers to court except where vital principles are concerned, such as payment.

The terms of agreement should be designed as a basis for a sound working relationship between seller and buyer: their aim should be to avoid misunderstanding by covering all areas of agreement and possible disagreement.

As a general rule, the lengthier the contract becomes, the more important it is to have a clause that allows the customer to sign while the salesman is with him, but to read it later.

The salesman should go through the contract carefully with the customer. Because it is a legal document, it frightens him.

Make sure he understands it properly. Answer the questions he is likely to ask, before he asks them. Prehandle any objections. Do not let him decide the definitions on his own. Otherwise he will be off to seek legal advice, and Christmas will arrive before the contract does.

Show him the special contract terms you offer. Emphasize them and the advantages they bring. Concentrate on making the decision easy for him.

Never, never make a call without your contract or order form on you. Even fill it out as far as possible beforehand.

Never send a contract through the mail unless you have had the chance to explain it to the customer earlier. And do not bring the contract up for discussion until the customer has indicated his intention to place the order.

Ask for the signature. Once he has taken up the pen to sign, do not say another word. You have said everything you need to say to take the order. Now you can only lose it by talking. If he asks another question, do not answer unless he shows that he will not sign until he has the answer. The customer will tend to talk while he signs, to shed some of the pressure he feels.

If there is any possibility that the customer will want more than one unit, try to get the other orders signed now. It will save you from having constantly to call back to get those signatures.

As soon as he has finished signing, without showing indecent haste, put the contracts safely in your pocket. Otherwise, he might just change his mind and tear them up. Then thank him, congratulate him on his decision, and leave. As with any call, it is important to know *when* to leave.

After the signature

After you have taken the signature:

- Thank him for spending so much time with you.
- Congratulate him and tell him he has made a very good decision.
- Prehandle any further questions he might have by showing him why they are not objections.
- If you feel his decision might be questioned by his colleagues after you leave, bring up the objections now and make sure he has all the answers at hand.
- Explain to him what he should expect your company to do. People are upset by what they don't expect, not by what they expect.
- Tell him that, if he ever needs anything or feels his problems are not being solved, he should give you a call right away. You are always there to help him. Make sure he has your telephone number.
- Mention some of the operating characteristics of the product, particularly those things that are important for successful operation. If you have a maintenance contract, point out the advantages of it to the customer but leave the decision to him. Otherwise he may feel you are giving him the bum's rush.
- When you have said everything you have to say, bid farewell and leave. You can only prejudice the order by hanging around.

14 Keeping the Customer Sold

Predelivery

If the customer cancels his order before delivery, the chances are that you have closed the sale rather better than you have sold the product's benefits. Don't telephone him and say he has signed and that is that. There is no value in threatening. It is bad business. The chances are that your company is not going to take him to court; and if he does not want to go ahead with his order, he can easily prevent delivery or stop payment.

The problem is probably no more than misgivings as a result of the sale. Treat them as you would a sale. Don't try to handle them over the telephone. Arrange another appointment. Find out what the real problems are and answer them. Go back to the last point in your original negotiation where you had agreement. Resummarize his criteria for ordering and restress the match between the requirements he is seeking and the benefits your product is offering. Close again. The chances are that he will withdraw his cancellation.

Selling is rendering a service, which means the customer gets what he thinks he has ordered, at a time when he has been promised delivery. He must also feel that the salesman is actively and successfully working to remove any obstacles.

It is the salesman's job to ensure that delivery of the product is made to the customer's satisfaction. His company should see that the customer is happy with it.

If delivery is expected later than promised, the salesman, as a matter of courtesy, should telephone the new date to the customer in advance, rather than leave him to find out for himself.

Don't make promises you cannot keep yourself. Among other things, that means making promises on behalf of your company. Broken promises are much worse than no promises at all because they break faith. In making any undertakings you have to make on behalf of your company, stress the probabilities of success and, perhaps, back up your statement with a third-party reference:

> "We appreciate that your requirement is for 24-hour service, and our average call rate is 20 hours. Many calls, of course, are very much quicker than this. Rather than ask me for promises I personally cannot keep, why not telephone Mr. Ansley of Kean & Company and ask him what our service is like in practice."

If you do make a promise or begin an undertaking, make sure you leave yourself enough time to carry it out.

No sale is ever completed with the signing of the order. Even if the customer will never sign another order with you, you must keep him happy because you will need his favorable third-party reference. If you know he should never have placed the first order, you should never have sold to him.

Remember, too, that the customer will inevitably feel some doubt when the product is first delivered. It can never be quite what he expected. So either on the delivery day or shortly afterward, make sure you call to handle initial problems and to reemphasize product advantages. Unless you do this, his colleagues may be only too eager to point out the weaknesses of his purchase; and once the customer is allowed to become disenchanted with it, the product will never do right.

Postdelivery

It is one thing to make the signatory happy. It is another to ensure that staff personnel who use the product are happy. It is flattering to them if you concern yourself with their requirements, and you can show them how to avoid many of the operational problems of your product. These people are most important to you if your product is to succeed in their company.

Similarly, if you have sold high in the company, it is important to resell to the man to whose department the product is going. If you don't, you run the risk that he will kill it just to *prove* that he should have been consulted in the first place.

Once the product is delivered, the threat comes from competition. To keep competition out, it is necessary to resell continually to the customer. This is done, not by stopping in for coffee and asking him how his family is, but by taking one benefit of the product at a time and re-selling it to him.

You must do this at least some of the time with the man who originally signed the order. It may be difficult to go back to him, but it is necessary. If you once managed to reach him and change his mind, the chances are a good competitor will be able to do the same.

If you get objections once the product is delivered, treat them each as a selling problem and handle them as you did objections in the sale. Don't just neglect them, even if they seem unimportant. That is the sure way to disaster.

At worst, your customer is a favorable third-party reference. At best, he will be reordering from you. So make sure you treat him well. Don't just sit on his back doorstep until he gets sick of the sight of you; but do make sure that, when he needs you, he knows where to find you. Then contact him regularly just in case he has a problem that is worrying him but that he considers not important enough to telephone to you about. Don't look for problems, though.

If equipment has been installed, or a product has been sold for further processing, it is important to call on the customer's premises occasionally to make sure the staff is happy with the operation. It will persuade the customer to believe that you actually care—and you should. No one should have higher standards for your product than you do.

Never try to handle complaints over the telephone unless they are normal calls for service. Arrange to call yourself immediately if the complaint is likely to be sensitive. If you fail to handle complaints personally and promptly, their importance can escalate and the customer can become antagonistic.

If the customer has a complaint, listen to it carefully and understand it. If it has no validity, show him why; but do not belittle him. He would not have mentioned it unless something was bothering him. Find out what it is.

If something does go wrong in delivery, installation, or operation, don't just apologize. It is solutions he wants, not apologies. Take over the problem, and get him the solutions. Telephone him back and tell him what you plan to do.

If your customer has too many service calls or bad deliveries, make sure you find out about them from your sales support organization and act on them before they become part of a more serious complaint from your customer.

A lot of customer complaints arise from bad original selling where the product fails to meet exaggerated claims made for it by the salesman. Never say, for example, your equipment *never* breaks down, or your deliveries are *never* late. Of course this is untrue, and the customer knows it. Even so, he will be down on you like a ton of bricks the moment the equipment or a delivery goes wrong.

Keep in mind that a product can still be performing the task for which it was purchased even when things are going wrong. For example, a truck-washing machine can still give the vehicle cleanliness the customer is seeking even when it breaks down frequently. Make sure you point out these benefits when you handle the customer's complaint.

Customer complaints should give you the chance to emphasize other benefits of your product or company, for example, the speed and skills of your service and sales support organization. They also present the occasion, where you feel it necessary, to impress on the customer the need for a minimum of product care and handling. Even the oil levels in his car must be checked occasionally.

If your company runs into a batch of difficulties, and your customers are complaining, remember that other supplying companies have similar problems too. Keep a proper sense of balance when you handle a customer's complaints and do everything you can to help him. However mad he gets, you can still be the supplier he wants to deal with.

Support your company at all times. Don't let yourself be pulled into talking it down. Remember, he is doing business through you and not directly with the company. If he starts to hear dismal stories from you too, he will see that all is lost and sever his connection.

If the customer wants to bawl you out, let him. There are no principles involved! Do not disagree with him. Do not interrupt him. Do not try to make a joke of it. Sit quietly, listen, and appear dignified but friendly. When you are quite sure he has finished, acknowledge what he has said and continue with your presentation. If he does not stop and looks as though he might throw you out, point out that this does not happen with all your customers, who are happy with your product, and that his problem too is capable of solution.

It could be that the customer is simply angry. In this situation it is useless for the salesman to try to persuade the customer that he is wrong to be angry. He may win the battle, but he will certainly lose the war. If the customer is angry, it is best to keep quiet and let the storm pass over. If it looks as though the tirade is flagging but the anger is still there, ask him *why*. Then, when he has nothing more to shout about, say to him something that is definite yet reasonable:

> "I'm sorry we've given you cause to be so upset. Obviously we cannot afford to let this happen to important customers like you, and I'm glad you've taken the trouble to tell me about it. I'll certainly take the matter up with my head office."

Treat all customers with equal care. Particularly, do not treat small customers cursorily when they are in the market for your product. You never know in selling where your next piece of good luck will come from; and, anyway, out of small acorns. . . .

Never—in this or in any other situation—swear in front of the customer or his staff. It can only lose an order, never win it. And if you must speak boastfully, be sure it is only about your product!

Finally, be familiar with your product but never with your customer. Always treat him with respect. Then you can never go wrong.

15 The Sale: A Summary

There is only one way to sell, and that is through face-to-face contact. It is only when you are physically in front of the customer that you have any chance of taking his initial order.

No one ever sells sitting alone in his office or at his home. If you are to sell to schedule, you must meet the required number of customers every week. This number is related to the number of orders you need in the sales period and your rate of converting calls to orders.

Plan your territory and your sales objectives, and then initiate control procedures to make sure you work to your plan. Use a little *mind* and be *effective.*

Business is a game. Selling and buying are part of the game. The rules are agreed upon between the players. The customer knows you are there to sell to him. Do not be embarrassed about it. He wants to be sold to by a professional, not by a fool. He wants to be absolutely convinced that he is making the right decision.

The trick then is to set rules for the game that suit your presentation. You have an initial advantage. You know exactly what your product offers. You know how you are going to approach the negotiation. You know the questions you are going to ask.

He has the disadvantage that he must wait to see your move. The answers he gives are answers to the questions you choose. While he is understanding you, he will freely undertake commitments when he does not know their importance. For you, these commitments are vital. Use questions like—

> "*If I* can carry out this operation more quickly and less expensively than you can do it now, *would you* be interested in my product?"

> "What are the reasons why you would not order my product at this moment?"

You can weight your presentation to influence the factors he will consider important in his future discussion. As the negotiation continues, you will be answering questions that reflect his commitment to these factors. In the final analysis you are in a position to say:

> "During our first meeting you said that if I could carry out this operation more quickly and less expensively than you can do it now, you would order my product. You've agreed that I can do it more quickly and that I can do it less expensively. I'd therefore like you to place your order now."

Words are important. Have a command of your presentation. Remember, it is not only what you say but the way you say it. Two words out of order can break the spell; and the sale is lost.

Go to every call properly prepared. Once you are there, don't let your own brilliance and *professionalese* overcome you. Talk straight to the man, talk sense, and talk business with the single objective of taking his order. Seek the information by asking questions that will construct your argument.

There is only one objective from the moment you shake his hand: to take his order for your product now. The *close* question is as good in the first sentence as in the second, and so on.

At every meeting it should be your single purpose to close the order across the table. Go high. You can always settle for a secondary objective, for example, to arrange a demonstration.

The customer will react favorably to good and truly vigorous selling. If you are sold something, you like to be well sold and convinced. Give that pleasure to the customer. However, be sure not to exaggerate your claims. They will only return to haunt you after the sale is made.

It is said that the salesman is never so good as during the first meeting. The first meeting has all the interest. The customer has the fascination of hearing something new. This interest can be turned into desire for your product, and closed.

Although the reasons to buy must be logical, the decision to make the decision is itself emotional. It can come at any meeting. The skillful salesman can make it come, recognize it when it is there, and close it. It is described as the *buying signal*. When it comes, stop whatever you are saying and ask for the order.

It is unlikely that the salesman will have to visit a customer more than four or five times, whatever his product—the introductory meeting, the demonstration, the site check, the order. A cold call from canvassing can add a call. Again, you might deliver the quotation.

Generally, it will take no more than these calls, plus two or three telephone calls. If you are taking longer than this, there is probably something wrong with your technique. You will begin to lose orders because people will think you are bothering them.

The customer will tend to be defensive. Everything he says must be analyzed for content. You must understand *what* he is saying, and *why* he is saying it. The reason for his statement contains the seed of the sale. Ask him *why* he made the statement, or *why* he asked the question. Only then can you provide the answers he needs.

The salesman is the expert in the market under discussion. The customer looks to him for knowledge. Because he has given so little and such inexpert thought to it in the past, he probably misunderstands quantitatively and qualitatively the dimensions of his problems. The salesman must therefore start at the very beginning and ask the questions that will identify the problem in its true form. Once the customer can understand the full dimensions of his problem, he will be able to appreciate the value of the product the salesman is offering.

At any human meeting, certain social formalities must be observed. You shake hands. You ask him how he is and comment on the day. It is the human way of doing what two dogs do when they meet, or two boxers who spar in the first round to gain the measure of each other. In business, these formalities are understood and should be reduced to a minimum.

In opening the interview, it is skillful practice to cause the customer to ask you about your product. The trick is to make him ask a question:

S. How do you do? My name is Lund. I have something here that is really going to fascinate you.
C. What is it?

Try to make the customer sit down before you speak to him. You need his full attention.

"Can we go somewhere where we are able to sit down?"

If he is standing, he can always start walking you out of the door.

The possible exceptions are at a demonstration or at a site call. Even here, it is not always a good idea to close the sale unless you know the customer will sign the agreement standing up. For a visual aid presentation, sit beside him.

Now you settle down to the game. In general terms, you state the subject and what you think to be its most important parts. You ask him questions for the information that will enable you to identify the most suitable form for your presentation to take. You ask him further questions to identify the exact requirements he is seeking to satisfy in his decision. But first you must identify the decision-making process in his company. Otherwise you could be playing with a second stringer:

> "If you think my proposal has merit, would you be prepared to put it before your next Board meeting, or would you be able to make the decision yourself?"

It is sufficient to unnerve the man who bluffs that he has the power of decision. The agreement by the right man is vital to the sale.

If you find you are with the wrong man, go back to square one. Find the real decision maker. You are with the wrong man if he says that all he has to do is to confirm the decision with another man. However simple he says it is, the other man is your contact.

Get away from the wrong man as quickly and as diplomatically as possible. At most, talk to him in general terms about what your product could mean to his company in the future. Talk to him in such a way that he is filled with commendable impressions of your purpose but has nothing with which to condemn you. Enlist his support in your scheme. He will want to identify with a project he thinks will be good for his company. Amazingly, too, he will not be upset when you go over his head.

Now you must interest your real contact. There is no need to try to be his best friend. You want him to respect you as a professional at your job. It is easier to say no to a friend than it is to say no to an expert, particularly when the weight of evidence is against you. That is the kind of pressure you want on him.

There are certain things that will always interest people—for example, nasty things about other people, talk about themselves, or talk about the things that are important to them.

Nasty talk about other people is too dangerous for selling. It interests, but that is all. The other people are usually the competition.

Speak well of competition. Otherwise you will create an albatross to wear around your own neck. He knows you think your product is better. So if you must speak of them at all, speak well of them. Tell him how good they are at so many things, but unfortunately not the things that are relevant to his particular needs. It can sound good if it is not glib. And praise will work against the competition, should they choose to speak badly of you.

Talk about him. Ask him questions about himself. People love to talk about themselves. Listen. Express interest in his company and in the range of decisions he has to make. Use the occasion to glean useful information. Raise him to your level. You are two men about to settle a problem.

Beware of opinions. They are interesting but they do not sell. They can only lose business. Do not just agree with him. Sound interested in what he has to say, but stay uncommitted. *Information that cannot be used for you can only be used against you.*

Ask questions. Open the questions with HOW, WHY, WHEN, WHERE, WHAT, and WHO. Ask him about his company. Ask him about the problems you know you can solve. Listen carefully to his answers, and the words he uses. Understand what he is saying and why he is saying it.

Guide and control him through every aspect of his requirements. Keep your questions tight. Mould and weigh his answers. Make him build the pedestal on which you will place your product. Remind him of his previous answers if he begins to drift.

Your product has certain physical characteristics out of which are derived a particular set of user benefits. Make him state his problem in terms of the benefits your product offers. Keep him to the point. Force him over each fence.

Summarize his statement of his problem and agree with him about it. Write it down if necessary. Confirm with him now that there are no other factors to be considered. Agree on the significance of the problem and the importance of an early decision. And trial close:

> S. *If I* can show you that my product will satisfy the requirements you have mentioned, *will you* be prepared to place your order for it?
> C. Of course.

Introduce your product. Tell him what it does and how it does it in words he can easily understand. You need only show that the product has the capability to do what you say it will do. Any technical information should be given in a consolidated form that he will understand and remember if he wants to tell someone else.

Use visual aids. They are really indispensable in selling. They should be put together within the logic of the sale and used fluently and confidently. They add weight and authority to your presentation. They build interest. Use pictures, products, graphs, and line drawings. They break the barriers between mental and visual understanding.

Paint word pictures. Go through the actions of having and using your product. Get up. Walk around his office if necessary—movement holds attention. Describe its made-to-order suitability, its trouble-free simplicity, and its ease of maintenance. Move from the general to the specific.

Sell benefits. If you talk of nothing else, talk benefits. If you state the quality,

"It is fast,"

state the benefit,

"It will save you time and money in operation,"

and the chain or related benefits:

". . . *which means* you will not have the additional expense of dirty trucks hanging around in the street, waiting for washing."

Ask him what each of these particular benefits means to him. Make him commit himself verbally to the benefits he thinks are particularly important to him. These are factors that will influence his emotional decision to buy. Question and destroy any points you think are irrelevant or dangerous. Add the one or two additional benefits that you know will weigh heavily in favor of your product. Then turn his statements back into direct questions for agreement:

"Do you agree, then, that this factor is particularly important to any decision you make in this area?"

Summarize to clarify and get agreement on each of the factors basic to the sale.

Personalize your presentation with the words *you* and *your*. It is what it will do for *you*. It is the great advantage it will bring to *your* company.

Couple *you* and *your* with the assumption that he already has the product:

"With the machine installed here, *you* will no longer have. . . . "

Talk about advantages, not disadvantages. He knows about disadvantages and will soon be able to pick them out (though you should prehandle those you know you will ultimately have to face by building the opposite case throughout your presentation).

The only disadvantages you mention are the ones that are really advantages. It draws him to you for your honesty and emphasizes the related benefit. Many product disadvantages reflect advantages of equal weight.

If he unearths your real disadvantage, you must provide the answer. Perhaps this disadvantage will not affect his particular operation, and if it does, it is small beside the advantages he will gain from using your product.

Control the conversation. Do not let him interrupt you unless you can derive unusual benefit from the answer. Even say to him:

"Do you mind if I come back to that point later?"

Control the ball. Make him play to you as you play to him.

Resummarize the benefits. These are the arguments for your product. Force them home as hard as you can. Make the comparison with the existing situation, if necessary in writing, column against column. Ask him which he prefers. Commit him to answers.

Show him the comparisons. After each one, get a yes out of him:

S. Would this be an advantage to you?
C. Yes.
S. Would this make your operation any easier?
C. Yes.
S. Would you prefer this?
C. Yes.

Yes, yes, yes. Then:

> S. Well, shall we go ahead and place your order for you? (*Silence*)
> C. Yes.

Yes becomes the easiest answer. You have helped him through his decision by forcing him to answer the critical questions for himself. You have given him the logic for the decision. You have also created the emotional environment in which he is able to decide.

Another technique at this point is to use a summary. After he has said yes, yes, yes to your questions, you return to a previous commitment he made:

> "You said earlier that, if I could satisfy you on these points, you would order the product."

Will he therefore place his order? Or, in case you feel there could be another objection lurking in the background:

> "Are there now any reasons why you should not place your order with me immediately?"

If the customer makes a no decision at this stage you might have built the sale on a false premise. Was there some basic information you failed to draw from him earlier in the sale? In this case you go back to the point of your previous agreement.

On the other hand, it might be some minor problem you can easily handle:

> "Could you tell me why not?"

If you have asked these questions and the customer continues to hesitate, perhaps by making insincere objections, you must confront him openly:

> "Can you tell me why you are not prepared to do business with me?"

The reason could still be quite simple and the solution well within your grasp. If the position is hopeless, ask one or two more questions to convince yourself, ask him if he knows any other company who might be interested, and leave.

The most important single word in selling, after yes, is *why*. If no is the answer and you have covered the ground, you must ask *why*. You must know *why*. Why requires an explanation. It throws the ball back to the customer. As long as you do not get to "because my father did because his father did," it is fair to follow up every subsequent answer with a *why* until you get to the answer vital to the sale. You have the right to the correct answer when he has caused you to spend time with him.

A salesman sells on objections. Logically, the customer would buy your product except for the reasons why he does not buy it. It is only when you know the exact reasons why he will not buy that you can show how the benefits of your product overcome his objections, or at least outweigh them if they cannot be overcome.

Selling is rather like trying to catch a mouse without a trap. If you try to lunge for him, the chances are that he will slip by and escape. Alternatively, if you continually reduce the amount of room he has to move in, he will ultimately hop into your hand.

To sell successfully, you must believe only two things: first, that your product is inexpensive in relation to the benefits it provides; and second, that there is no reason why the customer should not order it right away. If you doubt either of these things in your own mind, you will surely pass that doubt onto your customer.

Finally, do not oversell. You can easily lose an order by making exaggerated claims you cannot meet. (*A fool and his customer are soon parted.*) And do not undersell. You cannot lose the order you have not got, though you will lose it if you do not get it. And remember, *no* is never an acceptable answer in selling if the customer needs your product.

Index

AMACOM Executive Books-Paperbacks

Dudley Bennett	TA and the Manager	$4.95
Warren Bennis	The Unconscious Conspiracy	$4.95
Ronald Brown	From Selling to Managing	$4.95
Richard E. Byrd	A Guide to Personal Risk Taking	$4.95
Richard R. Conarroe	Bravely, Bravely in Business	$3.95
James J. Cribbin	Effective Managerial Leadership	$4.95
Saul W. Gellerman	Motivation and Productivity	$5.95
Bernard Haldane	Career Satisfaction and Success	$3.95
John W. Humble	How to Manage by Objectives	$4.95
Philip R. Lund	Compelling Selling	$4.95
Hank Seiden	Advertising Pure and Simple	$4.95
Leon A. Wortman	Successful Small Business Management	$4.95